WHEN SOMEONE YOU LOVE
HAS DEPRESSION

BARBARA BAKER is a freelance journalist specializing in health and self-help, as well as food, farming, organics and environmental issues. A member of the Guild of Health Writers, Barbara is currently freelance Health Editor of *BBC Good Food* magazine and writes for many other publications. In addition she is a t'ai chi instructor and volunteer telephone supporter for the charity Women's Health.

Barbara has recently gained a BA Hons from the Open University, a Diploma in Health and Social Welfare and Certificate in Health Promotion. She is currently studying for an MSc in Food Policy. Barbara's ambitions are to write television and radio drama, become an organic smallholder, and walk from Land's End to John o'Groats. Barbara lives in Cornwall and this is her second book.

Overcoming Common Problems Series

A full list of titles is available from Sheldon Press,
1 Marylebone Road, London NW1 4DU, and on our website at
www.sheldonpress.co.uk

Overcoming Common Problems Series

Overcoming Common Problems Series

Overcoming Common Problems

When Someone You Love Has Depression

Barbara Baker

First published in Great Britain in 2003 by
Sheldon Press
1 Marylebone Road
London NW1 4DU

British Library Cataloguing-in-Publication Data

A catalogue record for this book is available from the British Library

ISBN 0-85969-906-4

1 3 5 7 9 10 8 6 4 2

Typeset by Deltatype Limited, Birkenhead, Merseyside
Printed in Great Britain by Biddles Ltd
www.biddles.co.uk

Contents

Disclaimer

The author of this work has made every effort to ensure the information contained in this book is as accurate and as up to date as possible at the time of publication. However, medical and pharmaceutical knowledge is constantly changing. Readers should note that this book is not intended to be a substitute for medical or specialist advice. Neither the author nor the publishers can be held responsible for any errors or omissions or any actions that may be taken by a reader as a result of any reliance on the information contained in the text.

Barbara Baker has written this book in accordance with the guidelines suggested by the Mindshift 'mind out for mental health' campaign, co-ordinated by the Department of Health, in conjunction with the charity MIND (National Association for Mental Health), to stop the stigma and discrimination surrounding mental health, and to help to bring about positive shifts in attitudes and behaviour towards mental health.

For my dear nieces, Izzie and Lucy

Be kind and true to yourself and to others; savour the beauty of each new day; travel hopefully, and lightly; forgive yourself and others; trust your instincts; worry a little less and live a little more; believe in yourself, believe you *can* and reach for the stars, but be happy just to do your best. Don't compare yourself to others – be proud for who *you* are. Stand up for what you know in your heart is right. Respect all living things – we are all connected. With love.

1

What is depression?

Everyone feels sad from time to time. When things go wrong, or something upsetting happens, or we go through a bad patch, it's normal to feel down and our moods can vary from day to day. For most of us, most of the time, good days outnumber the bad ones and, once we are over the worst, we are able to carry on with our lives again. We are usually experts at knowing how to cheer ourselves up – by taking a day off work, seeing friends we like, watching a favourite film, having a lie-in, going to the theatre, taking a holiday, going for a walk, treating ourselves to some new clothes, or listening to music. But what happens when none of those things work? The expression 'I feel depressed' is now almost everyday language for 'I feel fed up', but depressive disorder, or clinical depression, is something very different.

Depression is an illness and is one of the most common reasons for consulting a doctor (*BNF*, 2002). No two people's experience of depression is exactly the same, but there are usually common features; whatever form it takes, though, it is normally extremely isolating, scary, lonely and debilitating. Depression can vary in severity from mild to severe, and can greatly interfere with an individual's ability to function, affecting family relationships, social life and working life. When you love someone who has depression it can be a worrying, frightening, tiring, draining and frustrating experience for you too, with the added heartache of seeing someone you care for enduring such a distressing time and perhaps not really knowing how best to help. Understanding more about the nature of depression can prepare you for this difficult experience and arm you with the knowledge you need about the ways you may be able to offer support and assistance.

The good news is that most people recover from depression – and for some it can even be a useful catalyst for change in their lives, learning to deal with negative events in a different way, for example.

How to recognize depression

Depressive disorder or clinical depression can be mild, moderate or severe and is also known as 'unipolar' depression. As well as mild or severe depression, there is dysthymic disorder, a less severe but typically more chronic form, which can last for two years or more.

The other main form of depression is manic (bipolar) depression and this is characterized by periods of depression alternating with periods of mania or elation. In addition, there is post-natal depression (see page 24) and Seasonal Affective Disorder (SAD) (see page 35).

Someone who has depression may not realize that they are depressed and it may never occur to them to seek medical advice. It is not always obvious to friends or family either; and even if you suspect a loved one is depressed, it's not always easy to tell just how severe that depression is or know how best to help. But depression is an illness – it is not the same thing as being lazy, weak, a wimp, or having a faulty personality. It is a medical disorder that can be treated.

Symptoms of depression

Doctors use a range of diagnostic tools to help them diagnose depression – for example, the American Psychiatric Association's classification in the *Diagnostic and Statistical Manual* (DSM IV) (American Psychiatric Association, 1994), the International Classification of Disorders (World Health Organization, 1994) or the Beck Depression Inventory (BDI). However, a new systematic review has pulled together and adapted the various criteria into a way that should make it easier for doctors to more easily diagnose depression and decide how severe it is (Williams *et al.*, 2002).

The symptoms listed are:

1 Depressed mood (dysphoria).
2 Anhedonia – if the person has lost interest in activities they would normally find enjoyable.
3 Sleep disturbance – if the person finds it difficult to sleep or needs to sleep more than normal.
4 Appetite disturbance or weight change – if the person feels the

need to eat more or less than usual or has unintentionally lost or gained weight within a period of about a month.
5 Decreased energy and feeling more tired after a minimum of effort.
6 Increased or decreased 'psychomotor' activity – if the person feels fidgety on a daily basis, can't sit still or, conversely, feels slowed down, as though treading in glue.
7 Diminished ability to concentrate or make decisions.
8 Feeling inappropriately guilty or worthless.
9 Recurrent thoughts of suicide – if the person feels life is no longer worth living or that they would be better off dead, or is preoccupied by thoughts of dying.

It is suggested that someone with a *major depression* would be expected to have five or more of the above symptoms, including depressed mood or anhedonia, every day or nearly every day for at least two weeks – causing 'significant impairment' in their social life, work life or in other ways; in other words, if the symptoms have adversely affected their home or work life.

Someone with a *'minor' depression* would be expected to have between two and four of the above symptoms, including depressed mood or anhedonia, every day or nearly every day for at least two weeks. Again, this would cause 'significant impairment' in their social or work life or in other important ways.

It is important to say that if the above symptoms can be accounted for by a recent bereavement, then a diagnosis of depression may be deferred.

Someone who had *dysthymia* would be expected to have three or four of the above symptoms, including depressed mood, on most days for at least two years. Symptoms of dysthymia include depressed mood, poor appetite or overeating, insomnia or sleeping too much, low energy, low self-esteem, poor concentration or indecisiveness and feelings of hopelessness. However, feelings of guilt and thoughts of suicide would normally be absent for a diagnosis of dysthymia to be made.

Someone who has *bipolar disorder* (*manic depression*) would be expected to alternate between a depressive state and a state of mania – for example, increased activity, talkativeness, less need for sleep, racing thoughts and constant, often unachievable ideas, inflated self-esteem or bouts of generosity, irritability, impatience and risk-taking. (You can read more about manic depression on page 6.)

Other symptoms of depression can include forgetfulness, tearfulness, feelings of inadequacy, feeling hopeless about the future, loss of motivation, reduced care over personal hygiene and appearance, loss of sex drive, anxiety and worrying about health more than usual. (You can read more about the symptoms of depression in Chapter 2.)

These are the most common symptoms of depression – though it is highly unlikely that one person would suffer from all of these. In isolation, any of these symptoms could have a variety of physical or other causes, and may be part of a 'normal' pattern of behaviour for some people. A doctor would look at the specific combination and severity of symptoms, coupled with how long they had lasted, to diagnose whether the person is suffering from depression, as well as to decide what form it takes and how severe the illness is.

Depression may be described as 'endogenous', which means it is not attributable to external events such as difficult life experiences, but more likely to be caused by, for example, biochemical factors; or 'reactive', which means it is more likely to have been triggered by external events. However, these terms are less commonly used nowadays as depression is widely thought to be due to a combination of causes.

Some practitioners dislike the terms 'major' and 'minor' depression as the use of the term 'minor' belies the seriousness of the illness to the person who is diagnosed with a so-called 'minor' depression, and it may also discourage someone who is diagnosed as having a 'minor' depression from seeking treatment. The terms preferred by some practitioners are 'primary' and 'secondary' depression. A 'primary' depression means the depression is not the result of any other medical or psychological cause, while 'secondary' depression refers to a depression known to be caused by a medical condition (such as an underactive thyroid) or psychiatric illness (such as schizophrenia).

These differences of opinion within the medical profession show that the way depression is diagnosed, what it's called, and how severe it is deemed to be, varies according to who is diagnosing it, the diagnostic tools they have chosen to use, and their own views.

There is no single 'right' or universally accepted way to diagnose depression, although in practice there would probably be broad agreement in most cases.

Case history: Carol
When my boyfriend was made redundant it seemed to hit him very hard. I knew when I met him that he had suffered from depression when he was younger, but in the seven years we were together I had seen no sign of it. It wasn't as if I woke up one day and realized Tom was depressed – it seemed to creep up on us bit by bit. At the beginning it just seemed as though he was really fed up and moody – in fact, initially he seemed more angry than depressed, even to the point of kicking doors. I'd never seen him like that before and, given the redundancy and how badly it had been handled by his company, I felt he was entitled to feel bitter.

In the first few weeks following the redundancy he did apply for other jobs, but then I noticed that he filled out application forms but didn't post them. After that, he didn't even look to see what jobs were on offer. He started to stay in more, and not want to go and see friends, and when friends came to us he would make an excuse and stay in the bedroom – saying he had a migraine. Much of the time he couldn't even talk to me. If I spoke to him it would take him an age to reply, as though everything was in slow motion. Gradually he became cut off from everything, his friends, family, social life. When he did speak, he kept saying that he would never get another job, and no matter how much I reasoned with him he just couldn't accept it. He was also convinced that he'd let me down, even though I constantly reassured him. It didn't seem to matter what I said, he just couldn't take it in. In the end, after I kept on at him, he saw a doctor and was prescribed antidepressants. He is not fully better yet, but he is much better than he was and I am hoping he might consider going to see a counsellor.

What is dysthymic disorder?

Dysthymia is a mild or moderate and common form of depression generally involving fewer or less severe symptoms, but for a longer period of time – at least two years. It is characterized by long-term, chronic symptoms (symptoms that recur again and again), which can stop the person enjoying or engaging fully with life or reaching their potential. Poor self-esteem and generally lowered mood is common, although in younger people it may be characterized by irritability and anger. If feelings of inappropriate guilt or suicidal thoughts are present, then a doctor is likely to diagnose depression, not dysthymia.

What is manic depression or bipolar disorder?

Bipolar depression (sometimes called affective mood disorder) is less common than other types of depression and is characterized by the contrast between extremes of mood – periods of depression followed by periods of 'mania' or elation. Sometimes the swings of mood are dramatic and sudden, other times they are more gradual, and much harder for the person – and those closest to them – to know where they are on a spectrum of behaviour. But it is not the same as someone who merely has 'mood swings'.

In the depressive phase of manic depression, symptoms will be the same kind of mix as those anyone who has depression might have. In the manic phase, there will be excessive 'highs' of mood and energy. These can manifest in a wide variety of ways – for example, talking constantly or very fast to the point where sometimes it is difficult to understand what the person is saying, irritability or outbursts of strong emotion such as anger, working too long or too hard, devising outlandish schemes, impulsive behaviour and loss of judgement – for example, making unrealistic plans; spending too much money or being over-generous, which can lead to getting into severe debt; staying up all night; taking risks with personal safety; eating or sleeping too little; behaving in an unpredictable way or doing/saying things that embarrass other people; behaving promiscuously; or feeling highly self-important with a constant rush of creative ideas. In very severe cases, hallucinations may also occur.

Someone who has manic depression may not always realize they are in a 'manic' phase, not least because they literally feel 'on a high'. The downside is that the manic behaviour can produce lots of 'undesirable' behaviour as well, and the person may afterwards be upset and shocked at things they have said and done.

Manic depression is sometimes associated with creativity. There is a long list of composers, artists and writers who are thought to have had manic depression, including Van Gogh, Tchaikovsky, Gauguin and Michelangelo, and the poets Tennyson and Shelley. The link is not clearly understood, except that in the manic phase many feel they can achieve anything, and this combined with high levels of energy and self-belief may, in someone who is talented, create a climate where they produce their best work.

Although women tend to be more susceptible to depression, a more equal number of both men and women are diagnosed with manic depression. Although some people only have one episode of manic depression in a lifetime, others have as many as four every year.

There does seem to be a genetic component to manic depression – the children of people with manic depression have a 5–15 per cent chance of experiencing it. If an identical twin has the disorder, then the other has a 70 per cent chance of having it too. Other contributing factors may be severe stress or emotional damage in early life.

The most common treatment for manic depression is a drug called lithium. It cannot cure the condition, but can control and help to prevent the worst symptoms.

How long does depression last?

It varies hugely between individuals, but can last anything from a few months to a few years, usually with remissions in between. People who are 45 or older tend to be more likely to have recurrent episodes. In general, depression is more common in elderly people – but depression is not a normal part of ageing. It is just as much an illness for an elderly person and just as treatable.

According to the World Health Organization, around 15–20 per cent of all people who have depression 'complete suicide' – but suicide is avoidable if people have the right treatment. (For more information about suicide, see Chapter 8.)

2
Understanding the symptoms of depression

We have already seen how wide-ranging the symptoms of depression can be. However, the two key symptoms in telling if someone is depressed are a generally depressed mood on most days, and/or a condition known as 'anhedonia', whereby someone is completely lacking in interest in what is going on around them and cannot take pleasure in activities they would normally find enjoyable. Someone who has depression – whether mild or severe – must have one of these symptoms, regardless of other symptoms they may or may not have.

How does a depressed mood and lack of interest manifest itself? This can be hard to quantify as every person is unique. Someone who is normally incredibly upbeat may have depression, but because they are normally so positive, their 'depressed mood' may seem on a par with what you might regard as a 'normal' attitude, mood and behaviour.

If you live with or are close to someone who you suspect may be depressed, then you will know what that person is normally like and it will be easier for you to spot a change, even if it is gradual. The kinds of things you might feel or say can be give-away clues that someone is depressed, for example:

'He just doesn't seem himself'
'It's as though she can't be bothered any more'
'He seems so listless at the moment'
'No one can persuade her to go out, she doesn't want to know'
'He looks sad all the time'
'She just wants to be on her own at the moment'
'He just stares into space'
'She looks so down'
'He can hardly get any words out'
'She isn't interested in anything any more'
'Nothing seems to make him smile these days'
'She always used to be so enthusiastic about life, but look at her now'

'He can't even get excited when the kids do something funny any more'
'She looks and sounds so lifeless'
'It's as though all the stuffing has been knocked out of him'
'She can't explain how she feels'
'I don't know what's wrong with him'
'I can't get through to her'
'He just looks depressed all the time'
'She can't seem to cope any more'
'He just sits there'
'She's oblivious to what's going on around her'
'He doesn't seem to care about anything or anyone'
'Nothing seems to cheer her up'

Let's look at some of the symptoms of depression in more detail:

- *Sleep problems.* For example, if the person finds it difficult to sleep or needs to sleep more than normal. Waking up very early and not being able to go back to sleep is a particularly classic sign.
- *Changes in appetite.* For example, you might notice the person is picking at food, insists they are not hungry, can't be bothered to cook for themselves, or forgets to go shopping for food. Or maybe they are uncharacteristically eating more – binge or comfort eating.
- *Tiredness.* Feeling more tired than usual is another typical symptom – wanting or needing to sleep, but also retreating to bed as a way of escaping or not having to participate in everyday activities. Or perhaps waking up early and not being able to go back to sleep, or apparently sleeping well but not feeling refreshed in the morning. You might notice a general sense of malaise and lack of energy and listlessness – the person may look and sound tired, be unable to keep their eyes open, or sleep at times unusual for them – mid-morning, for example. Notice any changes in patterns – such as wanting a lie-in when normally they would be bouncing out of bed.
- *Restlessness.* If the person fidgets all the time or suddenly it seems as if they can't sit still, or they find reasons to get up and walk around the room, or there is a sense they have to keep busy

all the time. Alternatively, they may seem much slower than normal, with slow reactions, a tired demeanour, and so on.

- *Inability to concentrate or make decisions.* If the person finds it difficult even to decide whether they want tea or coffee, or what to wear in the morning. They may continually respond to questions with the words 'I don't know'.
- *Feeling overwhelmed by the most simple tasks.* At its worst, even getting up to answer the doorbell can seem impossibly hard.
- *Feelings of guilt or worthlessness.* Worrying to excess about something they have or haven't done, or being overly concerned and troubled about what others think. Low self-esteem, feeling they haven't achieved anything, or that their life has been empty or pointless.
- *Suicidal thoughts.* Some people who are depressed say things like 'I'd be better off dead' or 'You'd be better off without me' or 'I wish I'd never been born' – these can all be signs that the person has privately had suicidal thoughts. That doesn't automatically mean they are seriously contemplating suicide, but it is a myth that someone who talks about suicide will not attempt it. Threats of suicide should never be ignored or dismissed as attention-seeking.

Other everyday symptoms of depression can include:

- *Forgetfulness.* At a mild level this can mean forgetting everyday things such as why they went into a room, or a person's name, or more serious forgetfulness like forgetting to pick up a child from nursery, or keep an important appointment. Also, forgetting birthdays or other important events, forgetfulness at work, and so on.
- *Tearfulness.* Crying for no apparent reason, finding it difficult to control tears in public places, crying at sad music.
- *Feeling 'spaced out' or having a sense of unreality.* Feeling 'unreal' or 'not quite all there' or 'not quite with it', light-headedness.
- *Feeling helpless or inadequate.* Convinced that nothing they do will count or is good enough. Feeling out of control of their life.
- *Feeling hopeless about the future.* Believing that everything is pointless and that no matter what course of action is taken, their life will not improve.

10

- *Feeling vulnerable or over-sensitive.* Perhaps over-reacting to criticism, feeling uncared for.
- *Loss of motivation.* Being unable to summon up enthusiasm or a reason for doing things.
- *Being unable to see the positive in situations or the joy in joyful things.* Being unable to appreciate, or being unmoved by, a glorious sunset, for instance.
- *Finding easy tasks more difficult than normal.*
- *A constant need for reassurance.*
- *Feeling useless or dwelling on past mistakes.* Agonizing over and over about how things might have turned out differently, constantly looking back and wondering 'what if?' Longing and pining for things to be how they were.
- *Being idealistic about the past when at the time they were in fact unhappy.*
- *Worrying about their health.* It is not uncommon for someone who has depression to be visiting their doctor more often with more aches and pains than usual, or real fears of serious illness.
- *Loss of sex drive.* Libido is typically low.
- *Feeling anxious about everything.*
- *Feeling irritable.*
- *Taking less interest in or care over personal appearance or hygiene than normal.*
- *Inclination to self-harm or take more risks than usual.* Driving too fast or doing dangerous things without care for personal safety – giving the impression they are on a 'self-destruct' mission.
- *Drinking more alcohol than usual.* This is often done as a way of trying to 'blot out' the pain or overcome feelings of isolation or social exclusion.

The complex nature of depression means that often it is the person who has depression who is the last to realize that something is wrong. Depression sometimes comes on very gradually, and if you are comparing yourself with how you were yesterday then there may be no obvious change, no big clue that all is not well. It is often easier for someone close to see the changes – although even then it's tempting to put it down to a 'bad patch' rather than an illness. 'Depression' is a big word, and for some it still carries a stigma. There are still many myths about depression too – such as believing that once someone has had depression they are always going to be depressed – so there are many reasons for preferring to believe that it's not depression at all, and delaying seeking help in the hope things 'sort themselves out'. Indeed, many people do recover from depression without any specific treatment, so this can be quite a complex issue. If you love someone who has depression, you may wonder if you should encourage them to see a doctor or not. But it would seem wise for the person concerned to seriously consider taking medical advice.

The stigma of depression

There is widespread stigma about depression and that can make it more difficult for someone to seek help even if they are aware they are depressed. It can also make it more difficult for family and friends to accept it. It is perhaps easy to understand why there is a stigma about depression. You can't 'see' mental distress in the same way that many physical illnesses are apparent. Some people associate depression and other mental distress disorders with weakness or madness, or being 'abnormal'. Some people think it is the same as, or caused by, stress – so do not regard it as an illness at all, but a more dramatic version of not being able to cope. Some people see it as a 'modern' affliction and have the attitude that people should 'just get on with it'. Or they may just assume it is attention-seeking. Many people have a kind of 'hierarchy' of illnesses – top of the list may be illnesses or conditions such as cancer or heart disease, but depression may be viewed as being far less serious or even totally dismissed. Such attitudes or prejudices are not necessarily malicious or deliberately unkind, but the result of ignorance, not knowing anyone who has had depression, or the result of fear of any kind of mental distress at all. It is hard to change strongly held beliefs – all you can do is focus on what depression means to you and do the best you can to get through this difficult time. It can help if you and others who are close to someone with depression are careful about the language used – for example, it is much better to say 'someone who has depression' rather than 'a sufferer of depression'. To describe a person as 'a depressive' also tends to be unhelpful – as though that person is wholly defined by their illness. It may seem picky, but language can be loaded with meaning and inadvertently give a misleading impression, which in turn may perpetuate prejudice by those who already have unhelpful attitudes.

3

What causes depression?

Studies suggest that a variety of physical, psychological and social factors cause, or contribute to, depression, so the cause varies from individual to individual, and the particular risk factors they happen to be exposed to or vulnerable to.

Physical causes include genetic make-up, biochemical factors (the chemistry of the brain itself), hormonal influences, seasonal factors (as in Seasonal Affective Disorder (SAD)) and illness or physical disease.

Psychological causes include stress, which may result from a range of difficult life events such as bereavement or divorce, adverse early childhood experiences, and the views someone may hold about themselves and their world. Strong emotions such as shame and guilt are often closely related to depression.

Social causes include the stress that may result from poverty, financial difficulties, unemployment, social isolation or exclusion.

These risk factors may vary in importance according to the age and gender of the person or how well they cope with stress. But it is the interplay of factors that is key – not everyone who is faced with a large number of difficult life events, and not everyone who is genetically at risk of depression, will actually become depressed.

Let's look at some of the causes in more detail:

Physical causes

Genetic make-up

Research shows that you are slightly more likely to suffer from depression if you have a first-degree relative who has depression, but it is not known why. It could be due to a 'genetic fault' such as a faulty chromosome or shared gene, but it could be partly because of a shared family environment. If genes are to blame, it is not known if it is one gene or a number of genes involved (Milligan and Clare, 1994; McGuffin and Katz, 1989).

First-degree relatives of someone who has bipolar disorder have a 10–25 per cent chance of experiencing a mood disorder – though depression, rather than manic depression, is more common (Gershon, 1990).

Brain chemistry

Scientists have discovered that depression is sometimes associated with low levels of particular neurotransmitters such as norepinephrine (also called noradrenaline) and serotonin (sometimes called 5-hydroxytryptamine or 5-HT). Neurotransmitters are chemical substances, which help to send messages to the brain.

Antidepressant drugs help to treat depression by ensuring that more of one or both of these neurotransmitters remain in the right part of the brain. (You can read more about how drug treatments work in Chapter 10.)

Another neurotransmitter thought to be implicated in depression is dopamine, known to be connected to the human response to pleasure; and it is thought that depression may involve too little dopamine. Some drugs, notably cocaine, mimic the action of dopamine to induce euphoria. Experiments on rats have shown that the brain releases dopamine before and after a dose of cocaine (BBC, 2003), but dopamine is still poorly understood at present and most drug treatments are based on altering levels of the neurotransmitters serotonin and norepinephrine.

Hormones

The role of hormones in depression seems critical too and the link between hormones, stress and depression is key. Robert M. Sapolsky, author of *Why Zebras Don't Get Ulcers* (see Further Reading), points out that when we think of someone who is depressed, we think of someone who lacks energy, but he says a more accurate picture is someone who is a 'tightly coiled spool of wire, tense, straining, active – but all inside'. In a way, the person is fighting an 'enormous, aggressive mental battle' and that inevitably means they have elevated levels of stress hormones. Stress hormones are activated when the body's 'fight or flight' mechanism is triggered. In addition to a surge in adrenaline, cortisol levels are raised. It works like this. One area of the brain – called the limbic area – is linked to our emotions and also affects the hypothalamus, which in turn controls the release of certain hormones. The hypothalamus secretes corticotrophin releasing factor (CRF), which in turn triggers the pituitary gland to release adrenocorticotropic hormone (ACTH), which triggers the adrenal glands to release cortisol and adrenaline. High levels of cortisol in the brain can cause mood changes and depression; and studies have shown that in depressed people, levels of cortisol are high. There has been much speculation as to whether raised cortisol levels actually cause depression or are just a consequence of depression. But it does seem that high levels of cortisol interfere with the amount of serotonin the body produces – and serotonin is a brain chemical (neurotransmitter) that has been found to be low in people who are depressed. Depression is also higher in people who have Cushing's syndrome, a condition where cortisol levels are high, along with symptoms such as weight gain, high blood pressure and skin that bruises easily.

There is a lot of interesting work on cortisol. For example, it is thought that the elderly may be more susceptible to higher cortisol levels; high cortisol levels may impair memory, but also in some way make an elderly person more susceptible to depression (Goodyer, 2003). The link with memory is interesting too. It has been suggested that people who have big gaps in their childhood memories seem more likely to become depressed as adults, although it is not known why. If memory gaps are linked to early childhood abuse or other negative experiences, it may be these that contribute to depression.

Hormonal disorders such as an underactive thyroid (myx-oedema), which is the result of a deficiency of thyroid hormone, are also linked to depression – that is, depression is more common in people with an underactive thyroid than in the population at large. Conversely, sometimes depression is suspected when in fact an underactive thyroid accounts for depression-like symptoms, so once the thyroid is treated, the symptoms improve.

Scientists still do not understand the precise relationship between depression and the various elements of the hormonal or endocrine system – the hypothalamus, the pituitary gland, the thyroid, the adrenal cortex and the various hormones that are secreted.

We do know, however, that excess thyroid hormone may produce manic symptoms in people with bipolar disorder (Lipowski *et al.*, 1994). It has also been found that women seem to be at higher risk of depression at those times of their lives most associated with hormones – menstruation, after giving birth, and during the menopause. Fluctuating oestrogen and progesterone do seem to influence mood – plus, they also regulate the metabolism of the neurotransmitters norepinephrine and serotonin. It is not known precisely how all these factors interact, but hormones certainly seem to play a part.

Illness

Some illnesses tend to be more associated with depression. This may be because the illness itself causes depression – hypothyroidism or Cushing's syndrome, for example. If this is the case, then treatment would be aimed at managing the underlying condition rather than the depression itself. Other conditions are associated with depression, but do not specifically cause depression – for example, diabetes, coronary heart disease, cancer and autoimmune disorders. Discovering you have a major illness can have a serious impact on morale and self-esteem, and adjusting to the loss of good health and the big changes that may have to be made as a result may be extremely stressful and emotionally debilitating. Other examples are conditions that cause pain – osteoarthritis or osteoporosis, for example – that is hard to cope with; or conditions like ME, which are psychologically challenging, and where the illness may not be properly recognized or understood by friends, family or the medical profession. Research also shows that depression occurs in about 50 per cent of stroke patients who survive for at least six months, and in half of these a major depression occurs. Sadly, someone who becomes depressed after a stroke does not seem to recover from the stroke as successfully as those who do not become depressed, and may be seen not as depressed, but as 'difficult'.

Depression is also more common in those who are disabled, those with a progressive condition such as Alzheimer's disease, people with head injuries, and those who have to undergo unpleasant investigations or treatments.

Medication

Depression may also be a side-effect of drugs being taken for a physical illness – beta blockers taken for heart problems, for example (Mulley, 2001). Other medications that have side-effects

17

that affect our mood, or make us more prone to depression, include drugs to lower high blood pressure, oral contraceptives and corticosteroids.

Someone who abuses alcohol or other substances is also statistically more likely to be depressed.

Psychological causes

Depression can also be triggered by what psychologists term 'stressors' – certain events, illnesses or other factors.

Unpleasant life experiences do not automatically cause stress: stress occurs when someone feels unable to cope with difficult events or circumstances, or there is a mismatch between the demands of a given situation and the resources and ability of a person to deal with it. So an event one person might find very stressful, such as moving house, might even be enjoyable to someone else. Take a simple example. If you have endured noisy neighbours for years and then have the chance of moving somewhere quieter, you are likely to cope much better with the hullabaloo of moving than someone who is forced to move away from a home they love to 'downsize' because they can no longer keep up the mortgage payments. Similarly, while divorce is clearly a stressful experience for most people, the stress may be less for someone who is supported by a wide circle of friends and family than for someone who has limited support. So psychologists are very aware that measuring stress is difficult because it very much depends on the previous experiences, expectations, support network and coping mechanisms of individuals.

Many important factors can feed into the way we cope with stressful events. For example, someone who has high self-esteem is more likely to believe they can cope if faced with a stressful series of events than someone with low self-esteem (Sarafino, 1990). A person who tends to have an optimistic outlook on life is more likely to see a stressful situation as a challenge and be determined to get through it than a person who has a very negative outlook.

A person's belief system is important too. Cognitive behaviour therapy (see Chapter 12) is based on the theory that our feelings stem from our thoughts and that we may build up unhelpful thought patterns and belief systems that influence whether or not we feel depressed. For example, if someone spends days preparing for a job interview, but despite being well qualified for the job and performing well at the interview is then rejected, they may react in two different ways. While one person may take the rejection in their stride and resolve to do better next time, someone who held the belief that they were useless and unemployable might be very distressed and completely knocked off balance by the experience. Aaron Beck has suggested that early experiences with parents, siblings, friends and others in our lives can prompt us to adopt negative thinking patterns (such as 'I'm no good at anything' or 'No one could ever love me') that they then hold on to as adults, despite evidence to the contrary. Such faulty thought processes can affect behaviour and relationships and make someone more prone to becoming depressed.

The timing of stressful life experiences can be a key factor too. An accumulation of stressful experiences within a short space of time – two or more bereavements within weeks or months of each other, or a range of stressful experiences within a short time frame, for example, losing one's job, a bereavement and relationship breakdown all within a six-month period – may also influence how one copes.

Another factor is a person's sense of control over their lives. Someone who feels powerless to control stressful events is more likely to feel stressed than someone who is able to make changes to lessen the stress involved. If someone falls behind with their mortgage repayments and receives a letter from the lender threatening repossession of their home, they are more likely to feel in control and less stressed about the situation if they know they have funds coming in that will resolve the problem, than someone who has no way of earning any more money and has other debts they can't pay. When someone feels at the mercy of events and circumstances beyond their control, they are more likely to feel stressed.

One psychologist, Martin Seligman, came up with a theory called 'learned helplessness', which he suggested was a key characteristic of depression. The idea is that if someone feels trapped and unable to improve their situation or control their lives no matter how hard they try and over a long period of time, then

19

they 'learn' to become helpless, they become apathetic, and may even stop trying to make improvements in their lives because they are convinced that, whatever they do, they simply won't be able to make a difference. If you try to do something and repeatedly fail, then self-confidence plummets and depression may result (Seligman, 1975).

Other psychologists have different theories. Heinz Kohut argued in the 1970s, for example, that depression results when people are disappointed by relationships and are no longer able to feel positive about their own achievements and self-worth (Gilbert, 1992).

Many psychologists have shown how someone who is a victim of neglect or abuse as a child, either physical or sexual or both, may be more prone to anxiety and a mood disorder in later life – and also be more vulnerable to depression in later life (Gilbert, 1992).

Many personality traits seem to be connected with depression. People who are desperate for approval, obsessed with achievement, or tend to be highly self-critical, can all be at risk of depression if life goes in such a way that for some reason others don't approve of them, they don't achieve what they want, or they fall short of their own high expectations. Depression is especially likely if life events make someone feel ashamed or humiliated (Gilbert, 1992).

Shame and guilt are emotions strongly associated with depression. Someone may feel ashamed about their appearance, size, or their sexual orientation. Survivors of sexual abuse, rape or incest may wrongly believe that what happened might be their fault. Guilt can also stem from having fallen short of one's own high standards, having done something the person considers wrong or is perceived to be wrong by others, having made the wrong decision, or not doing something they think they should have done.

Lewis Wolpert, author of *Malignant Sadness* (see Further Reading), says in his excellent book that in his view depression is 'almost always related to sadness due to loss of some sort or another – money, personal relationship, social status, job or security', but exactly who gets depression may be influenced by a genetic predisposition. The theme of 'loss' has been highlighted by others – for example, two researchers called Brown and Harris in the 1970s. They studied women aged 18–65 in south London, all of whom had a depressive disorder. Brown and Harris said that loss and change were the key features of most events bringing about clinical depression. Losses included the death of or life-threatening illness of a partner, child, close relative or friend, a child leaving home, marital breakdown, a plan or threat to separate, or discovering an affair. It was also noted that women who had suffered the loss of their own mother during childhood were more likely to develop depression in adulthood. Although Brown's and Harris's work has met with some criticism, loss, disappointment and change do seem to be important factors in the onset of depression (Brown and Harris, 1978).

Dorothy Rowe, author of the excellent book *Depression: The Way Out of Your Prison* (see Further Reading), says that depression is something 'we create for ourselves and just as we create it, so we can dismantle it'. Rowe believes that people who are depressed tend to have one or more of a range of views they believe to be true, such as that it's wrong to get angry, that they are essentially bad or valueless, or that they can never forgive others or themselves. Rowe looks at the barriers to coming out of the 'prison' of depression, such as fear of rejection, and offers ways of changing one's perspective.

Jon Kabat-Zinn, author of another superb book, called *Full Catastrophe Living* (see Further Reading), says that sooner or later the accumulated effects of stress, compounded by inadequate ways of dealing with it, 'lead to breakdown in one form or another'. He adds that what gives out first will depend to a large extent on your genes, your environment or aspects of lifestyle. 'The weakest link is what goes first,' he says. So if you have a strong family history of heart disease, then you might have a heart attack. For others it's the immune system that is vulnerable or the digestive tract. But for some it is their 'psychological resources' that are vulnerable, so a 'nervous breakdown' or depression may result. Kabat-Zinn's approach to combating depression is 'mindfulness' – a moment-to-moment awareness that allows you to choose how you deal with stress and to control how you react in different situations.

All these approaches seem to align closely with the principles of cognitive behaviour therapy, which you can read more about in Chapter 12. What they have in common is the idea that even someone who is ill can choose how to think – and by changing how they think they can have more control over their illness.

Richard Carlson, author of *Stop Thinking and Start Living* (see Further Reading), suggests that one approach is to stop thinking altogether! 'If you begin to see that your thoughts ... are just thoughts and as thoughts they can't hurt you – your entire life will begin to change today,' he says. He takes the cognitive therapist's approach that our thoughts determine how we feel, and advises that thinking about problems only makes them worse. It may be one reason why women tend to be more prone to depression – we tend to analyse everything more than men!

But some things actually help protect us against stress and depression – good social support from those around us, feeling loved and cared for, part of a social network whether it's a family or a church group, a strong sense of self-esteem, knowing others hold you in high regard, feeling you have some control over the things that happen in your life, that you can make decisions and take action to make things better for yourself, having a positive attitude, and feeling that you can succeed and be effective if you want to, and being resilient – someone who copes well with change and is not thrown off track by minor setbacks.

4
Who is at risk?

Depression is an illness and, like most illnesses, can affect absolutely anyone. According to MIND, the National Association for Mental Health in the UK, one in five people will suffer from depression at some point in their lives and, worldwide, major depression is now the leading cause of disability; therefore it is much more common than most people realize.

According to the World Health Organization, depression is more common in women than in men. It can affect people of any age, though the highest incidence is in middle age. More and more young people have depression too. According to the World Health Organization, anxiety and depressive disorders commonly occur together.

Depression in women

In general it is thought that depression is twice as common in women than men, although it is not fully understood why. The difference may be partly attributable to women being more willing to seek medical help than men. However, genetic and biological factors and hormonal changes in women as a result of age and reproductive cycles are all likely to be important influences too; in children, depression seems to affect equal numbers of boys and girls, but the rates change after puberty. We already know that women are more likely than men to suffer mood swings as a normal part of the menstrual cycle – and some women do have their first experience of depression within a few months of giving birth.

But other gender factors can play a part too – sociologists point to the greater stress women are often under because of the demands of the conflict between their traditional role as wife and mother and pressure to work, or the desire to have a career as well. Lewis Wolpert, in his book *Malignant Sadness*, says that women do not seem to experience a greater number of distressing life events than men, but may react to them with greater intensity. He points out that when in emotional distress, women are perhaps more prone to 'excessive self-analysis', talking about what's happened to friends, crying, writing a diary, and so on, while men are more likely perhaps to ignore their problems altogether, play sports or drink alcohol. Depression is also more common where there is domestic violence.

Post-natal depression

According to the Association for Post-Natal Illness, post-natal illness affects between 70,000 and 100,000 women and their babies every year in the UK. Many people confuse the 'baby blues' with post-natal depression, but there is a marked difference between the two conditions.

The baby blues affects about half of all mothers. It starts within two to four days following the birth of a child, generally lasts for a few days, and then disappears. It is characterized by feeling emotional, tearful, crying for no apparent reason, and finding it difficult to sleep. Feelings of anxiety, guilt, fear and vulnerability are common too. The most likely cause of the baby blues is hormonal changes, coupled with sheer tiredness and the emotional impact of the birth. It is distressing for the mother and for family and friends who witness it, especially as having a baby is supposed to be a joyful experience; and after all the excitement leading up to the birth, it can be hard to handle, especially if the baby is well and there appears to be no real reason to feel down. Fortunately, the baby blues are usually short-lived – if a mum is allowed to have a good cry without being made to feel guilty or ashamed, given lots of love and reassurance and allowed to rest, the baby blues should pass after a few days.

Post-natal depression, however, is a more serious condition affecting up to one in ten mothers. It may not start until a few days after the birth or may come on between four and six months after the birth, which is why it often goes undetected as many people assume that post-natal depression starts as soon as a baby is born. It can last for months, or even years, and may never be suspected throughout that time. Onset may be gradual or it may appear very dramatically and very suddenly. A woman may have post-natal depression only after her first child and/or after a subsequent child.

Many of the symptoms of depression described in Chapter 1 can occur in post-natal depression – tiredness, feeling unable to cope, irritability, loss of appetite and sleep problems, as well as anxiety, loss of interest in sex and difficulty concentrating or making decisions. Other symptoms may be a general feeling of hopelessness and despondency, worries about being an inadequate mother or not loving the baby enough, crying all the time, panic attacks, fears about the baby's health or her own health, and a sense of being out of control. Some women suffer from obsessional thoughts or worry they might harm the baby.

One problem is that all new mothers may to a much lesser extent be expected to feel tired, anxious about being a good mum and worried about their baby's health, so post-natal depression is often missed or not suspected. Many mums with post-natal depression are wrongly told that 'all mums feel like this' or that it will pass – or it is assumed that hormones are to blame and that this is normal and just something to be put up with.

Of course, many new mums do find the experience, especially first time around, more difficult than they imagined. There are new skills to learn and it can all be a shock to the system. In addition, getting up in the night to see to a baby can result in disrupted sleep and acute tiredness as a result. Many new mums are completely unprepared for finding that they don't seem to have a minute to themselves, and then feel guilty because when their partner comes home it seems they have little to show for the day, especially if they haven't got round to doing routine chores, making a meal, etc., despite best intentions. Some mums even find to their horror that they simply don't seem to have time to have a decent shower, let alone a long soak in the bath. And the role of a woman is such that it takes a very 'new man' to appreciate that a woman who stays at home to look after a baby has a full-time job just doing that, without the extra household chores, cooking and cleaning that she may be expected to do on top. These all may sound trivial things to anyone who hasn't experienced them, but can build up and up to a real pressure point.

In addition, there is a huge potential loss of independence and sense of isolation to contend with. If a woman has had a career or a job she enjoyed and now finds herself at home all day with only a baby for company, it may be a major culture shock. However much the baby was wanted and is loved, it is still a big change to adjust to. Visitors may come and go, but may be mainly interested in the baby, not the mother. This is understandable, but can add to the isolation and frustration a new mum feels. New motherhood can feel very unrewarding when you are giving up so much for a tiny bundle who may cry non-stop. Just the feeling that you can no longer decide anything on the spur of the moment, but have to consider the baby, along with all the trappings of babyhood – which weigh a ton and take ages to organize into the buggy or the car – can sometimes make it seem too daunting to bother, and the joy of being able to do your own thing seems lost for ever. Loneliness can be an issue too – if you are used to being out at work or having a busy social life, and suddenly the nearest you get to stimulating company is watching daytime television, then it can seem very lonely. If you don't happen to know other young mums and are stuck at home all day, it can seem that, overnight, you are trapped. If your old friends have lost interest in your new baby, the effort involved in meeting other new mums locally can seem an ordeal. Confidence can ebb away as your world seems to get smaller. A stay-at-home mum who is used to a career may also find it very difficult to come to terms with what they see as loss of status and financial independence.

Having a baby can change the relationship between a woman and her partner too – and underlying tensions surrounding different priorities, different needs and new pressures can emerge as a mother gets used to her new role and the losses and gains it involves. This may be compounded if the woman is too tired for sex or her libido is low. And it can herald problems with other family members where none existed before – everyone has views on how best a baby should be brought up, and if a mother or mother-in-law decides to give her the benefit of their vast experience it can be very daunting, especially if the new mum is still trying to adjust and decide for herself what works and what doesn't. Conversely, if the new mum lives away from parents, lack of support from other family members may be the issue.

All these problems can seem worse given the fact that everyone expects a new mum to enjoy being a doting parent, ready to sacrifice all her own needs for the new arrival. If a mum has been looking forward to the birth but then finds she doesn't feel the kind of instant bond of love she was expecting to feel, this can be a huge shock and lead to terrible guilt and disappointment. She may feel she can't voice her true feelings in case she is thought to be a bad mum, incompetent, selfish or ungrateful. So the feelings become submerged and unexpressed.

Case history: Laurel
I can't remember a time when I didn't want children – it was something I looked forward to even throughout my early teens. I met my partner and we married when I was 26 and we started trying for a baby almost immediately. When nothing happened, I panicked for a time, thinking that perhaps something was wrong, and I became increasingly distraught at the thought I would never become pregnant. Then when I eventually fell pregnant, 18 months into the marriage, I was overjoyed.

I didn't have an easy pregnancy, but still I enjoyed every moment of it. I had the birth planned down to the last detail, we got a beautiful nursery set up, everything. When my daughter Georgia was born I noticed straight away that I didn't instantly feel all the things I thought I would. I put it down to the stress of getting to the hospital on time and just feeling exhausted. But the weeks went on and I didn't feel much different. My husband had taken two weeks off work when I got home with the baby, but when he went back to work I began to feel panicky.

Friends came in and out and my dad came to stay for three days, but I felt as though I was not really there. My mum had died from breast cancer four years before, when she was only 47, and I missed her so much. I think I was still grieving for her in a way too. Then suddenly this tiny bundle was there all the time, every second of the day, and I couldn't handle it. I felt so guilty, so ashamed. All my friends knew how much I'd wanted a baby for years, so I was trying to keep up the pretence. I felt I'd let everyone down.

There were days when I would get out of bed to see my husband off to work and then go straight back to bed and drag myself up five minutes before he was due home, doing the bare minimum for the baby. Fortunately, she was a really good baby and was content to sleep all the time, but I still worried I was neglecting her. I fantasized about having Georgia adopted and the feelings of disgust about myself welled up. I just didn't want her. I wanted everything to be the way it was, but all the time I was trying to put on a brave face. I couldn't tell anyone how I felt because I was so ashamed. My best friend instinctively knew I was struggling and offered to help by babysitting and giving me some time away, but I couldn't admit how I felt even to her.

I just felt a weight of responsibility and I didn't feel ready for it. I had gone on so much about motherhood and now I hated it. Some days I would cry for hours on end, going through the motions of changing and feeding Georgia, but resenting every moment I spent with her. At the same time I was very worried about the harm I might be doing her and was convinced she sensed my resentment.

In the end it was my health visitor who realized I was ill. She was fantastic and suggested I talked to my GP about it, and he immediately referred me to a counsellor. My feelings didn't change overnight, but gradually I became more my old self and my love for Georgia began to grow. I look back now and realize I was ill and I have forgiven myself. Georgia seems none the worse and I am planning to have another baby.

According to MIND, a new mother is more likely to become depressed if she has no one to confide in, no work outside the home, and three or more children under 14 years of age living with her. Women who were separated from their own mother before the age of 11 for an appreciable length of time – either because of illness, death or being sent away to boarding school – are also more vulnerable to post-natal depression. A new mother may not realize that she is feeling depressed because of something that happened during her own childhood, but if past hurts have been submerged and unspoken about for years, becoming a mother may somehow trigger an unleashing of raw and frightening emotions. What many people don't realize is that it is never too late to address those past hurts, with the help of a sympathetic counsellor, look at them in a safe atmosphere, and get in touch with the deeper feelings and anxieties that they still exert until you are finally able to let go of them and move on.

One study conducted by midwives suggested that post-natal

depression may be a natural reaction to the loss of a woman's pre-parenthood self – effectively, the new mother is mourning the loss of her independence. The midwives felt that new mothers are often unprepared for the emotional and practical implications of mother-hood and are too often misled by idealistic images – so that when reality bites they feel guilty for not being perfect, angry at what they have lost, and often isolated and lonely too (*Observer*, 2003).

The good news is that post-natal depression can be treated. Counselling can help, so too can looking after emotional and mental health. And if you are living with someone who has post-natal depression, especially if you are the partner of someone with this illness, there is a tremendous amount you can do, not just from a practical viewpoint – sharing the workload around the house, for example – but emotionally too.

A more severe form of post-natal depression is 'puerperal psychosis', which is fortunately very rare. This condition normally occurs within a few weeks of the birth and usually comes on suddenly. It may start with severe restlessness, elation and inability to sleep, along with mood swings between lows and highs; hallucinations and delusions are also possible, with disturbed behaviour that may require a stay in hospital. One episode of puerperal psychosis does not automatically mean a woman will experience it if she has another child. Someone who has a previous or family history of mental health problems may be at a higher risk of developing this condition.

Helping someone with post-natal depression
If you think someone you love could be suffering from post-natal depression then it is important to get medical help. She may find it useful if you attend a doctor's appointment with her. Here are other ways you could help:

- If it's your partner, tell her you love her – she probably feels very vulnerable and unlovable at the moment.
- Try to understand what she is going through – having a baby is a huge event for a woman and a big change in her life. However much the baby is wanted, there are still adjustments to be made.
- Encourage her to talk about how she feels, not just to you and to a doctor, but also to friends, her health visitor or a counsellor.
- Ask how you can help – could you take on more domestic

responsibilities to share the workload for a bit? It may seem to you if your partner is at home with the baby all day and you are out at work, that compared to you she doesn't have much to do – but she may find being at home with the baby overwhelming.

- Listen to others – friends and other members of the family who voice their concerns to you about your partner. They may see things you haven't noticed that they are worried about or she may confide in them and not in you.
- Make sure she has proper, regular 'time off' from the baby so she can have a long soak in the bath, go shopping, see a friend, and have the occasional night out or do something she wants to do by you taking full charge of the baby – and make a good job of it so she can properly relax!
- Pay attention to her as well as to the baby – it sounds obvious, but at a time when everyone naturally coos over the baby, Mum can often feel left out.
- Don't nag or point out the things around the house that haven't been done. Don't criticize her ability as a mother, and if she is paying less attention to her appearance than normal, realize that this can be a symptom of the illness – making adverse comments will not help the situation.
- Don't tell her to 'pull herself together'.
- Suggest other sources of support such as a self-help group – talking to other mums who feel the same way – or contacting a specialist organization such as the Association for Postnatal Illness, or MAMA, the Meet-a-Mum Association (see Useful Addresses).

Treatment options in post-natal depression
The best treatment may be a combination of the kind of practical and emotional support you and other family members and friends can give, together with counselling. Antidepressants can help, but may not be appropriate for a woman who is still breastfeeding. For more information about counselling and antidepressants, see Chapters 10 and 12. It is important to remember that post-natal depression is an illness – and mothers who suffer from it do get better.

The Association for Postnatal Illness advises that the contraceptive pill may cause depression in some women, and if a woman is depressed after birth it may make the situation worse. It would be a good idea to discuss this with a doctor, but at the same time ensure adequate birth control is used.

Depression in men

Although depression tends to affect women more than men, depression in men is more likely to be 'hidden', and men are more likely to kill themselves as a result of depression. Suicide is the most common cause of death in men under the age of 35. It is often harder for a man to admit he has the kind of emotional or other problems that might lead up to a period of depression. Men are often brought up to think it is wrong or wimpish to show their feelings, let alone cry. Men tend to be more competitive than women and are conditioned to aim high, to be powerful, successful and the breadwinner, even in this enlightened age where women are supposed to be equal to men. And that can mean men try to hide their depression even from those they love most. Often men don't have anything like the same kind of support network that a woman might. Women tend to have a wider circle of friends they can moan to, share feelings with, talk over worries with, than men do. Even if men have lots of friends, they may tend to talk about sport rather than about feelings. It is much harder for them to admit they are having problems or feeling vulnerable, and they don't want to appear weak or needy or admit they need someone to lean on. A man may also find it difficult to accept he is suffering from depression at all, and perhaps is more likely to try to put symptoms down to some other cause or physical illness.

If a man does admit he is depressed it can be hard for his partner to accept this. Some women want a 'new man', but when it comes to the crunch they actually find it difficult to acknowledge that their man isn't a tough guy after all, and has weaknesses and vulnerabilities like everyone else.

According to the Royal College of Psychiatrists, trouble in a marriage is the most common problem connected with depression in married men. Often men do not know how to handle relationship problems and are more inclined to 'switch off' or withdraw, which can leave a woman who wants to 'sort things out' feeling frustrated, ignored and angry. In turn this can lead to conflict, which can escalate to the point of a marriage break-up. Unfortunately, men are about three times more likely to kill themselves than women – and men who are separated or divorced are more likely to kill themselves than single men.

One problem is that men tend to be more reluctant to consider counselling or psychotherapy than women, even though it could be of enormous benefit.

Depression in children

Up to 2.5 per cent of children aged 6–12 may have a major depressive disorder, with boys and girls at equal risk. After puberty the rates climb to the same incidence as adults, with girls twice as likely to become depressed as boys. Children are more likely to appear irritable than depressed, and bored rather than sad.

Major depressive disorder does run in families, so children are more likely to develop the disorder if one or both of the parents have it. However, various studies suggest that the start of depression in children is not triggered by genetic factors alone, but accompanied by other triggers such as family conflict, abuse or major losses.

A depressive episode in children tends to last between 8 and 13 months (Kovacs et al., 1984, and Goodyer et al., 1997) and 50–59 per cent recover by the time they are followed up, although up to 70 per cent may experience a recurrence (Poznanski et al., 1976, Asarnow and Bates, 1988, Birmaher et al., 1996, Emslie et al., 1998, McCauley et al., 1993, and McGee and Williams, 1988).

Children who are depressed tend to have more behaviour problems and are at higher risk of alcohol and other substance abuse later on. But childhood depression can be treated with a combination of antidepressants and cognitive behaviour therapy or psychotherapy. Interestingly, tricyclic antidepressants have not been shown on the whole to be any more effective than a placebo, but it is not known why, and an antidepressant of the SSRI type (see Chapter 10) is often the first choice of treatment, although the results are not wholly convincing either. It is best to discuss treatment options carefully with a doctor if your child is depressed.

It is easy to assume that children can't have 'real' problems and to dismiss their worries and fears as 'childish' or of far less seriousness than an adult's simply because they are children – yet a child's fears and worries are just as real to them and just as valid, and should be treated just as sensitively.

Depression in adolescents

It is notoriously difficult to tell whether a teenager who appears to be permanently fed up or has problems with sleep, appetite and mood swings is just being a 'normal' teenager or suffering from depression – and there has been relatively little research in this area so that even psychiatrists do not agree. As well as genetics and other factors such as conflict with parents or major losses, the hormonal changes associated with puberty are thought to be a key factor. Many children and adolescents tend to show signs of anxiety before depression sets in (Kovacs *et al.*, 1989). Many children and adolescents are also disruptive – though it is not known why the two are linked. It seems unlikely that having behaviour problems causes depression – but children who have behaviour problems may be more likely to come from a family with more problems at home than other children, a fact that also puts them at risk of depression. We just don't know (Kovacs *et al.*, 1989). What we do know is that most depressed adolescents recover, though some go on to develop depression as adults.

Apart from family problems and genetic factors, outside stressors such as bullying at school may contribute to depression too. As with young children, research currently suggests that tricyclic antidepressants (TCAs) are not an especially effective treatment, and selective serotonin reuptake inhibitors (SSRIs) are more likely to be prescribed. (For more details on these drugs, see Chapter 10.) Again it is not clear why – it may be there has been insufficient research to date, trials have not been sufficiently well designed to show efficacy, or the drugs just don't work. However, cognitive behaviour therapy (see Chapter 12) has been found to be useful, particularly for adolescents with mild or moderate depression (Kovacs *et al.*, 1989).

Depression in mid-life

We have all heard the term 'mid-life crisis' and it has perhaps become a bit of a joke, yet depression in mid-life is a debilitating illness. Adult women are twice as prone to depression as men and it is thought that apart from hormonal influences, the strain of being a young mother may take its toll, along with the loss of financial independence and other social factors (Paykel and Kennedy, 2003).

Rates of major depression in mid-life are the highest among married women, but – interestingly – higher in men who are single, widowed, divorced or bereaved. This suggests that while women may find juggling a marriage, home, children, and career a strain, men are cushioned from depression if they are married – perhaps because it is so often the woman who takes on most of the burden (Paykel and Kennedy, 2003).

Depression in mid-life can be triggered by many events – this is the time when so many changes can occur: people move house; change jobs; marriages break up; parents become ill and may need caring for; children grow up and flee the nest, leaving an empty void; parents and friends may grow old and die; and then there are physical changes to contend with too – decline in physical fitness, changing appearance, the menopause for women, and the prospect of old age.

Both antidepressants and cognitive behaviour therapy have been shown to be effective (for more information, see Chapters 10 and 12).

Depression in old age

Contrary to popular opinion, depression is not a normal part of ageing. On the other hand, the kind of life experiences that tend to occur as one gets older do seem to be linked to depression. For example, bereavement or life-threatening illness, either in oneself or someone close to us, appear to be risk factors that can make someone susceptible to depression (O'Brien and Thomas, 2003). To complicate matters, depression is more likely in illnesses more readily associated with older people, such as cancer, heart disease and strokes. Depression is itself a significant risk factor for the subsequent development of coronary artery disease and heart attacks. Studies seem to indicate that depression in older people tends to be more common in those who live in residential care homes.

On the other hand, many older people are reported to feel satisfied with their lives (National Institute of Mental Health). Nevertheless, 3 per cent of the over-65s suffer from clinical depression.

There seems to be some expectation that old age is automatically associated with higher rates of depression, and that may be why there is some evidence that depression in old age is not routinely treated – although there is no reason why treatments, whether drug treatments or counselling or both, cannot help. So if the person you love has depression, it's important to know that there is no reason why depression in old age shouldn't be treated successfully (Wattis, 2001).

Graham Mulley points out that sometimes depression goes unrecognized in older people who are medically ill (Mulley, 2001). Some people feel their depression is just a normal part of ageing, and so don't like to make a fuss. They may consider psychological symptoms to be of less importance than physical symptoms – or assume the doctor will think so. If they have a major health problem such as cancer, they may feel that mentioning how they feel emotionally will detract from the care they need for their physical illness – and they may not know that depression can be treated. Some people may not even realize that they are depressed. Others complain of physical symptoms – stomach or head pains, for instance – which may mask the psychological symptoms.

Studies have shown that antidepressants can be effective, so too can cognitive behaviour therapy and other talking treatments.

Seasonal Affective Disorder (SAD)

This is a form of depression that affects some people during the winter months. Most of us feel better on a bright, sunny day – and would admit to wanting to stay tucked up indoors on very cold, miserable days. But Seasonal Affective Disorder is diagnosed when symptoms seem directly related to the reduced hours of daylight.

But why does light – or the lack of it – affect mood? When light hits the back of the eye – the retina – it helps messages to pass to the hypothalamus, the part of the brain that governs sleep, appetite, mood, sex drive, and how active we are. Reduced levels of light can slow us down in all these areas, yet the exact cause of SAD is still not fully understood. Low levels of the neurotransmitter serotonin and higher than normal levels of the hormone melatonin are also possible factors. The Seasonal Affective Disorder Association (SADA) estimates that SAD affects around half a million people every year between September and April, and in particular during December, January and February. Around 20 per cent of people with SAD suffer a mild form of the illness, and this is called subsyndromal SAD or the 'winter blues'. For others, SAD is a more disabling illness and requires treatment.

Typical symptoms of SAD include depression, low levels of energy, an increased need to sleep, feeling lethargic, poor concentration, irritability and low motivation, as well as anxiety, loss of libido and mood changes. Some people tend to crave carbohydrates during this time; others suffer from a weak immune system and become more vulnerable to infections. According to SADA, you are more likely to start getting SAD between the ages of 18 and 30 – but it can affect anyone.

Most people with SAD probably never seek treatment and may only be vaguely aware that they feel down during the winter months. A small number of people experience symptoms so severe that they find it difficult to function properly without treatment. Diagnosis can normally be made if a person suffers symptoms for three or more consecutive winters. Ironically, it may be the partners of people with SAD (or others close to them) who spot the pattern of symptoms and their connection with the time of year, long before the person who has the disorder – so you may be able to encourage them to seek advice.

Fortunately, it has been shown that light therapy – regular daily exposure to full spectrum light via a special light box during the winter months – can improve symptoms for approximately 85 per cent of those with SAD and the results are rapid. Many people see improvements within three or four days. Light therapy involves being exposed to a very bright light – about ten times the intensity of normal domestic lighting – for between one and four hours a day. The person with SAD can carry out normal activities such as reading or eating while in front of the 'box'. In the UK, boxes are not available on the NHS and have to be purchased from specialist retailers.

SADA believes that antidepressant drugs like the tricyclics (TCAs) are not always helpful for those with SAD as they can worsen sleepiness, although non-sedative SSRI drugs (which increase levels of serotonin) may be effective if used in conjunction with light therapy. (For more details on types of antidepressant drugs, see Chapter 10.)

5

The link between psychological stress and depression

When we are stressed the body's 'fight or flight' mechanism is activated, preparing us either to fight or run away from danger. The autonomic nervous system is divided into the *sympathetic* and *parasympathetic* nervous system. The sympathetic nervous system is concerned with all the automatic responses of the body. For example, when faced with danger, the digestive system slows down so that blood is directed to the muscles and brain – obviously it is more important in an emergency to fight or run than digest food. Breathing gets faster so as to supply extra oxygen to the muscles, the heart speeds up, and blood pressure rises so blood is rushed to the parts of the body that need it most – to run or fight. Muscles tense, ready for the person to run. Sugar and fats pour into the blood to provide an instant energy boost. Hormones are elevated too – norepinephrine and epinephrine (more often known in the UK as adrenaline) are released to help increase the heart rate and blood pressure and release stored sugar respectively. Cortisol is also released – cortisol can break down lean tissue to convert to sugar to help provide energy.

If all this happens in a genuine fight or flight emergency, then our body responds as it should. But if it happens when we are sedentary and because the stress isn't a real fight or flight situation (as in being charged at by a raging bull), but instead is mental and emotional or psychological stress (fuming because you are stuck in a traffic jam is a simple example), then it can be very harmful for both physical and mental health.

One way we can learn to handle stress is by working *with* the parasympathetic nervous system – this branch of the nervous system effectively gives us the chance to put the brakes on the fight or flight mechanism by use of relaxation techniques.

But what counts as stress? Two psychologists, Holmes and Rahe, have come up with a ranking of life experiences (called the 'Social Readjustment Rating Scale') and a score based on the stress each event was liable to cause (Holmes and Rahe, 1967). One purpose of this was to give psychologists a tool to see how far stress was related to illness.

The rankings were as follows:

Rank	Life event	Mean value
1	Death of spouse	100
2	Divorce	73
3	Marital separation	65
4	Jail term	63
5	Death of close family member	63
6	Personal injury or illness	53
7	Marriage	50
8	Fired from work	47
9	Marital reconciliation	45
10	Retirement	45
11	Change in health of family member	44
12	Pregnancy	40
13	Sex difficulties	39
14	New family member	39
15	Business readjustment	39
16	Change in financial state	38
17	Death of close friend	37
18	Change to different line of work	36
19	Change in number of arguments with spouse	31
20	Large mortgage	31

The more stressful events from the list that a person has within a short space of time, the greater the stress they are under; and several psychologists have shown how people who have had heart attacks or other health problems have had high scores using this scale. The scale has its critics, but it may be a useful way of thinking about the person you love. Have they endured several of the experiences on this list within a fairly short time frame? It may help you understand better what they are going through and what might have led to the depression. Of course, everyone has different stress thresholds. Someone who is rarely anxious, tends not to worry, and is renowned for being laid back is less likely to become stressed than someone who is a worrier and less able to take setbacks in their stride.

If someone is not able to easily express difficult or negative feelings about events such as bereavement or divorce at the time they happen, they may become depressed later on as unexpressed emotions build up.

A recent survey by the Samaritans in the UK shows that 59 per cent of those surveyed report being stressed more than once a month – with the middle-aged (defined as those between 35 and 54) most liable to be stressed out. The most recent MIND survey (MIND, 2003) shows that 45 per cent of those who have felt stressed in Britain have been depressed as a result (Samaritans, May 2003).

Major life events are some of the most common triggers for depression. If you love someone who has depression or is vulnerable to depression, it may help to think about how these experiences may have affected them. Loss and change are dominant themes – losses invariably involve change of one kind or another while change is often stressful. Below are some common life experiences, some of which may be triggers for stress or depression; in some instances there are ideas as to how you might be able to help.

Bereavement

Losing someone you love or care about is for many the most traumatic experience of their lives. As well as deep sadness about the death itself, bereavement can bring a frightening mixture of emotions and feelings – sadness, fear, loneliness, anger and guilt. All these emotions are natural and part of the grieving process, though not everyone experiences exactly the same pattern of grief. The symptoms of grief can seem very similar to symptoms of depression – and grief can sometimes develop into depression. In some cultures in the Western world, grief is often a hidden process. We don't tend to wail in public or show emotion, even at a funeral. Much of it goes on behind closed doors in a bid to 'stay strong'. All too often we regard crying as a kind of weakness instead of a beneficial and positive display of emotion. We hear people say things like 'He's bearing up well' as though it's a good thing not to cry. We see others cry so infrequently that when they do we don't know how to cope and become embarrassed or feel awkward. Yet crying is a natural reaction to loss. Trying to hold back the tears isn't necessarily a sign of strength, and it can make a person's journey through grief more difficult.

Some emotions are stronger than others and can be quite frightening in their intensity. Anger is common – the anger at the waste of a life, anger with the dead person for being in the wrong place at the wrong time, not caring enough about their health, smoking or drinking too much. Anger about being left alone to cope, or anger with oneself for all the things that we may believe we 'should' have said or done, anger about those things we or they *didn't* say – not saying 'I love you', and so on. Other emotions are often present too – the 'pang' of pining for the person who has died.

Colin Murray Parkes, author of one of the best-known books on bereavement, *Bereavement Studies of Grief in Adult Life*, talks of the 'stages' of grief and how numbness, the first stage, gives way to pining and despair before recovery takes place. Parkes points out that depression, feelings of panic, persistent fears, nervousness, fears of nervous breakdown, loss of weight, reduced ability to work, fatigue, insomnia, trembling and nightmares are all features of 'normal' grief. In other words, feeling depressed after a close bereavement is absolutely normal.

But a bereavement can lead to depression for a variety of reasons. Sometimes if grief is delayed because someone is unable at the time of the bereavement to show their grief and the feelings turn inwards, depression can result.

How long does it take to get over the death of a loved one? It is impossible to say. Everyone is an individual and it very much depends on the person, who it is they have lost, how close they were, what kind of relationship they had, whether they were able to prepare for the death, the circumstances of the death itself, and how able they are to express their emotions afterwards. Some people may begin to feel 'back to normal' after six months, but two years and longer is much more common.

It is easy to underestimate the impact the death of a loved one can have. If you are concerned about a son or daughter or brother or sister who has lost a partner and seems to be depressed, you have probably seen first-hand the agony they are going through. Apart from the sheer shock and loss and all the emotions of grief they are going through, there is the awful pining for the dead person, the loss of emotional closeness they once had, the loss of a physical closeness, and on top of all that the endless practical problems that need to be coped with in order to ensure financial stability as well as keep a home going. If they have children, there is all the worry of how to cope with their grief too. Then there is the difficulty of coping with friends and family. Often people don't know what to say to someone who has lost a partner, so far from being a support in a time of crisis they may become an additional problem instead. And just being alone throughout the ordeal can mean the bereaved person goes for days without talking to anyone – the kind of non-communication that can set the scene for the onset of depression. One reason why losing a partner can result in depression for some is the totality of the 'investment' a person has placed in the partner who has died. Psychologists find that widows or widowers who were completely dependent upon their partner in almost every way fare much worse after their partner dies than those who enjoyed activities and had friends of their own (Persaud, 1997).

There are additional problems in the case of a violent or unexpected death. Some people become preoccupied with the details of how someone died, only to find they then cannot get unpleasant visions out of their mind. For some it is important to have a sense of 'closure' – someone deprived of seeing the dead loved one after death, for whatever reason, may feel angry and cheated. The ritual of being able to see the dead person may seem gruesome to some, but can bring enormous relief and help the grieving process for others. The ritual of a funeral can help the grieving process for many too.

It is important to stress that there are many cultural differences when it comes to death, dying and the grieving process – what may be appropriate or desirable in one culture may be quite different from what happens in another and this may be a significant factor if the person you love who is depressed is from a culture different from your own, and may require great empathy, respect and understanding on your part. It will help you enormously if you find out as much as you can about the cultural differences, and if you wish to offer help you will then be able to do so with more sensitivity and awareness.

The death of a child is the most profoundly sorrowful experience any parent can have. It goes against every parent's hopes and dreams to outlive their child under any circumstances. The tragedy of losing a baby to sudden infant death syndrome, a young child to illness or an accident, an adolescent or any child in any circumstances. Knowing how to help someone after the loss of the child is particularly difficult.

In general, someone who is grieving does not usually experience a loss of self-esteem, as is the case with depression.

What you can do for someone who has been bereaved:

- *Be there.* Often it is a help to be with someone who is grieving, even if they don't feel like talking. Just being there, allowing them to feel your closeness, to know that you care, is a help.
- *Don't be afraid of tears.* A grieving person may feel they want to break down and cry but can't bring themselves to do so, even in front of those they love most and who love them most. The fear of breaking down can lead to that person cutting themselves off and becoming isolated. Showing them that you can cope with their tears, and are perhaps able to cry with them, can be a blessed relief. If they do cry, resist the temptation to try to encourage them to stop crying. Let them cry. Hold their hand or touch their arm. There is no need to speak. Show your acceptance that it's OK for them to cry.
- *Don't be afraid to mention the dead person.* It is true that some people don't want to be reminded of the person they have lost, although this may be because they have not yet come to terms with the death. If you show you are not embarrassed to talk about the deceased, the bereaved person may be glad of the opportunity to talk naturally about them.
- *Be a good listener.* Allow the bereaved person to talk freely about his or her thoughts. Sometimes people have a real need to say the 'unsayable' – things on their mind that they would like to express, but feel afraid to or don't know how to.
- *Be patient.* Another crucial aspect of helping someone to grieve

is to allow them to go over and over the details or circumstances of the death. This can be wearing if you feel it has been said many times before, but psychologists who are experts in grief believe this is a very important part of the grieving process and helps someone to come to terms with, or find a meaning in, what has happened.

- *Be prepared for strong emotions.* Giving your time and allowing them to set the pace will help. So often we tend to say things like 'Don't think like that' or 'Don't say that' when people express guilt or anger or other difficult emotions. We do so in a bid to help; trying to help the person to stay positive may *feel* like the best thing we can do – yet allowing them to express those difficult emotions may be even more valuable.
- *Offer practical help.* If you can, offer help and mean it. People often say 'Is there anything I can do?', but it is difficult for someone in need to respond to a vague offer like this. So think of specific ways you really could be useful. Could you, for example:
  – go with them to the hospital to help with the ordeal of picking up the dead person's things?
  – help with funeral arrangements?
  – ensure they have food in the fridge that they can easily heat up (as they may not feel like shopping and cooking for themselves for several weeks)?

Case history: Jackie
It took me a long time to get over the death of my mum. When I went to a bereavement counsellor in a state and she asked me how long ago my mum had died, I think she was astonished when I explained it was over two years ago. I had been 'stuck' in my grief and become depressed as a result. There were so many things I felt guilty about and it was eating away at me.

The bereavement counsellor enabled me to get it all out, all the things I couldn't share with the rest of the family. I think there was a built-in expectation by the family that we should just get over my mum's death as soon as possible and be normal again. My brothers and sisters didn't want to talk about the nitty-gritty or hear me splurge my emotions all over the place, so there was a lot buried inside me, festering away. My family tend to be the sort of people who like to 'stick to the facts', and it is a cardinal sin to be fed up, worried or upset – anyone who dares to show any kind of emotion is written off as 'over-reacting'. It was only after finally talking it all through with the counsellor, which was such a tremendous relief, that I was able to begin to move on and come out of the depression.

Divorce or relationship problems

It is hardly surprising that divorce ranks so highly on stress scales. No one gets married and expects a marriage to fail. We start with hopes and dreams and are carried along on the romantic crest of a wave, deeply in love and convinced we will stay together, no matter what the hardships or problems, determined to be happy, forsaking all others. If it goes wrong, it can be devastating. Whether it is because a couple have simply fallen out of love and grown apart, or because one partner has discovered the other has been unfaithful, or whether outside pressures have helped to drive a wedge between them, divorce is a sad, stressful and scary time. It is often stressful even if it is what both parties are sure they want. Dividing up assets, deciding who gets what, trawling through old photo albums and dividing up the pictures, seeing how happy you used to be together . . . it is all incredibly traumatic.

We know from statistics that in the UK that the number of divorces is now rising, with 157,000 marriages ending in divorce in the year 2000 (Census, 2001). In 2002 alone, Relate counselled 95,000 clients. Relationship problems do not necessarily lead to depression, but can be a trigger factor for some. Discovering your partner has been unfaithful, coping with their drinking, or verbal, physical or sexual bullying, arguments over the children or money, finding you no longer have the same hopes and dreams, or nothing in common any more . . . relationships falter for a wide variety of reasons. As emotions such as anger, bitterness, resentment and hate build up, communication breaks down. The less easily someone is able to deal with a foundering relationship and put it right, and the less outside support they have, the more susceptible they may be to depression.

When a relationship is in trouble, the thought of separating and making a new life can seem impossibly daunting. It can seem 'easier' to go on living with the pain of an unhappy relationship, even though it keeps us locked into a spiral of despair. If one party doesn't even want to break up or get divorced, or is reeling from the shock of their partner's infidelity, and all the feelings of rejection that inevitably go with that discovery, it is hardly surprising that it can lead to depression in some people. To discover one's partner has had an affair is a tremendous shock and deeply difficult to come to terms with. If a woman feels she has been 'traded in' for a younger model or one partner discovers the other has been secretly seeing someone else for a long period of time, the bond of trust is broken, and the feelings of betrayal are extremely traumatic. And along with strong emotions of anger may come self-pity, self-blame and, despite it all, an unquenchable pining for the relationship that used to be, a longing for it all to be the way it was, incredible sadness for what has been lost, even love for the person who seems to have betrayed you.

If divorce proceedings then follow, feelings may turn more towards anger or revenge; and when it is all over and the person has to face life alone, sheer loneliness and a sense of isolation.

How you may be able to help

It can be very frustrating trying to help someone whose relationship is in difficulty – especially if you take the time and trouble to respond to their anger and distress, yet they seem to ignore your advice and stay in what is clearly an unhappy relationship. But the fact that people do stay in unhappy relationships is a measure of how extraordinarily difficult it is to leave.

The sense of failure, fear of the strong emotions that will inevitably be involved if a separation or divorce ensues, losing one's home, joint friends, the possible uprooting from a particular area and the social structures someone has spent time building up over years or decades, the financial implications, the prospect of feeling guilty afterwards, the ordeal of trying to make a new life for oneself, the effect on one's children and likely difficulties about access . . . all these factors can make staying in an unhappy relationship by far the lesser of two evils.

It is hard to see someone you love struggling to come to terms with relationship difficulties, break-up or divorce. One of the best ways to help is to be on hand to listen – the emotions they are going through are similar to those suffered by someone who has been bereaved: denial, numbness, sadness, anger, pining for the person who has left them. The need to go over the details of the marriage and what led to the break-up of the relationship may be strong. The sense of loss and suffering can be enormous. Just to be there for them may be a great help, a willingness to listen empathetically to what is said, without judging or necessarily even trying to 'say the right thing' until the person feels it is all out of their system – a process that may take many weeks and months, or even years. Sensitivity to their loneliness will help too – finding a balance between allowing them to talk it through and helping them to keep busy, remembering to invite them for social occasions without feeling the need to 'pair' them with a member of the opposite sex, and in particular remembering that occasions such as Christmas (the holidays) or birthdays and anniversaries are likely to be especially hard for them. When such complex emotions are rife, it is these simple acts of kindness that count so much.

If your partner is depressed and you feel it is partly due to the fact you are experiencing relationship difficulties, you may feel guilty, angry, or unsure what to do. Talking to a counsellor may be a tremendous help to anyone experiencing relationship difficulties – and is an option well worth exploring. (For more information about counselling, see Chapter 12.)

At the beginning of a relationship, when we are in love with someone, it seems as if we are blind to his or her imperfections and full of optimism about the future. A couple in love long to be with each other constantly, and it seems inconceivable that anything could sever that strong bond. And for many, even when the thrill of romantic love fades and the reality of everyday existence settles into mundane routine, the relationship endures.

It is very hard for outsiders to ever fully know what is going on in someone else's relationship. If the person you love is depressed and you think it is connected to difficulties in their relationship, there is likely to be little you can do. You may have spent huge amounts of time listening sympathetically, giving advice, being at the end of a phone to offer support or guidance, and yet still feel your contribution hasn't made a difference. You may feel powerless to help – frustrated that you have given advice that has been ignored, angry that despite your best efforts nothing has changed, and that you haven't been able to help put things right.

Childhood experiences

Someone who has been abused or neglected as a child may be at more risk of depression. Paul Gilbert, in his book *Counselling for Depression* (see Further Reading), suggests that some common early life themes seem to emerge with regard to depression. Counsellors find that those who are depressed have often had problems with their parents or upbringing in some way. For example:

- Parents who simply weren't there, either because they were ill, had divorced or died.
- Parents who were physically there, but unable to give emotional support – perhaps *their* parents were cold or distant.
- Parents who were abusive, which adversely affected the child's ability to trust or form good relationships with others.
- Parents who were overly critical or controlling, which made it more likely that their child would be sensitive to feeling guilty and blaming themselves when things went wrong.
- Parents who were overly demanding or actually tried to compete with their children, making the child grow up feeling inferior.
- Parents who seemed to prefer one child over another, so that the less favoured child felt they weren't good enough.
- Parents who were always arguing or threatening to leave the children.
- Parents who were unpredictable, particularly if mental illness was a problem.
- Parents who were needy, putting pressure on the child to become a 'parent' rather than be the child.

Family problems

There are as many types of 'family problem' as there are families; and circumstances that one person might find stressful may present no problem at all to someone else – depending on their own personality or ability to deal with friction, how sensitive or assertive they are, how involved they are, and so on. So it is very difficult to generalize. Stressful family problems can arise in all kinds of ways – for example, coping with parents, siblings or children who:

- Don't get on or argue all the time.
- Drink too much.
- Get in trouble with the law.
- Take drugs.
- Have financial problems.
- Are violent.
- Are verbally abusive.
- Are sexually abusive.
- Are over-controlling or over-protective.
- Don't seem to care about us.

Some events seem to exacerbate problems in some families – weddings, holidays, funerals, special occasions. There are endless permutations.

Coping with family problems is not easy. Many of the situations mentioned above are highly complex in their own right and it is not possible to go into detail about each. Counselling may give the person a chance to talk through their feelings and devise new coping strategies.

Stress or problems at work

According to the Royal College of Psychiatrists, in any one year about three in every ten employees will have a mental health problem – and depression is one of the most common. Tell-tale signs that someone is depressed in their workplace include:

- Taking more time off sick than usual.
- Not turning up or being late for meetings.
- Working more slowly than usual.
- Making more mistakes than usual.
- Being unable to cope with criticism from superiors.

- Inability to concentrate.
- Forgetting to do things.
- Failing to complete tasks on time.
- Disappearing for longer stretches of time than normal – longer lunches, longer times spent in the toilet.
- Withdrawing from colleagues or general office life, wanting to be on their own.
- Getting into arguments uncharacteristically.
- Avoiding tasks that normally they would enjoy or cope with – such as talking on the telephone to customers.
- Not eating properly – or comfort eating.
- Inability to make decisions or delegate.
- Staying late at the office to 'catch up'.
- Taking work home.
- 'Rehearsing' tasks before they need to be done – for example, writing down what needs to be said in a phone call or worrying about what they will say in a meeting.
- Crying for no apparent reason.
- Feeling overwhelmed by tasks they would normally cope easily with.
- Becoming more pedantic than usual about non-important things.

If you don't work with the person you love then it may be impossible to know if their depression is affecting their work unless they tell you. But these symptoms – one or several – are likely to be in addition to symptoms you have noticed yourself at home or in your everyday contact with them.

It may be that difficulties at work have actually helped to trigger the depression in the first place. Some possible triggers include:

- Being bullied by colleagues or superiors.
- Feeling isolated from colleagues for some reason – for example, if they have to work in a remote office away from most other colleagues.
- Feeling ostracized by colleagues in some way – if no one wants to sit with them in the canteen, for instance, or they are left out of invitations to the pub.
- Having too much work to do.
- Having lots of deadlines to adhere to.

- Feeling a 'round peg in a square hole' – for example, finding that they have to give presentations or take the lead in meetings when they find speaking in public very difficult.
- Having too little work to do.
- Feeling their abilities and skills are undervalued or unrecognized.
- Being over-promoted and feeling overwhelmed by the responsibility involved, or unsure of their ability or competence to do the work.
- Being under-paid for the work in comparison to other people.
- Finding the work unsatisfying – for example, if it is routine, mundane or repetitive.
- Feeling insecure about the permanence of a job, particularly if the person has family commitments or is under financial strain, or is worried about the possibility of a contract not being renewed.
- Poor physical work conditions – too cramped, dirty or noisy, in an environment that is too hot, too cold or smelly, or where there are poor toilet facilities, or working in an office with no natural light.
- Difficult or long commute to work.
- Being made redundant or being sacked. According to the Royal College of Psychiatrists, up to one in seven men who become unemployed will develop a depressive illness within six months.

None of the above are automatically triggers for depression – what one person finds hugely stressful is a minor irritation to someone else. We all react differently to stress, and an accumulation of stressors – particularly if someone feels vulnerable or has other problems either in the workplace or on the home-front – can all combine to build up to a pitch where depression is more likely to result.

How to help someone who is depressed at work:

- Being there as a sounding board to help someone talk through problems they face at work is likely to be one of the most helpful things you can do. This isn't necessarily as easy as it sounds. For example, if it's your partner who is depressed, and they work in a specialized industry, their work environment and their role in it may be highly complex. If you have never talked in depth about what their work involves, know little of the kind of culture that operates, and don't know the various personalities involved, it can be hard to get a handle on what exactly is going on and why it has become stressful. Finding out will require really good listening skills on your part – as well as having a feel for the right questions to ask. For the person under pressure, it can feel like an added stress to have to explain their working situation and environment in minute detail to someone who isn't familiar with it – and someone who is depressed may feel unable to make the effort involved to explain all the ins and outs. Yet if this can be done at an early stage, then it could be enormously beneficial for that person to know they have someone close to them who really understands why they are finding it difficult, why they are feeling under pressure; and perhaps be able to maintain an objective standpoint, offer ideas for new approaches or how to tackle specific difficulties.

- Another way to help is to do your bit to ensure the person gets some kind of balance in their life. Someone who is stressed at work may be 'taking their work home with them', worrying about it, and finding it more difficult to pursue outside interests or maintain a social life. Being there to go out to the cinema or theatre, or play badminton or go out for the day at the weekend, could be a great help.

- You may be able to encourage the person to make changes at work that will help to make them feel better. For example, if they feel overwhelmed by the quantity of work, and they are lacking in self-esteem or confidence, they may feel very awkward about asking for help or delegating tasks. Talking to a line manager might be a first step. Discussing this kind of nitty-gritty detail and helping them to feel they have options could be very valuable.

- You could also encourage the person to seek help. It may be there is, for example, a workplace counsellor, or an occupational health service or union representative who could offer guidance. Everyone's circumstances are different, but it is worth at least finding out if there are opportunities to get help at work.

- Talking about taking time off work is another option worth exploring – but though time out from workplace stress may help in the short term, if the underlying problems are not resolved it could make things worse – particularly if work is piling up while the person is away.

- Encouraging them to seek help outside work could be valuable too – finding a counsellor who specializes in workplace stress, for example. (For more details about how to find a counsellor, see Chapter 12.)
- Another option is to look at specific areas where adding on skills might help – could a course in assertiveness training help, for example? Or perhaps a series of sessions with a cognitive behaviour therapist would help. (For more information about cognitive behaviour therapy, see Chapter 12.)

Coping with bullying at work
A survey carried out by the Institute of Personnel and Development (IPD) estimates that one in eight people have been bullied at work in the previous five years, causing stress and depression in some.

Bullying at work can come in many guises – if bullying behaviour is consistent over a sustained period of time, then it can take a real toll on physical and mental health. How is it possible to recognize a bully? All the following are typical bullying behaviour. A bully in a position of authority may:

- accuse an employee of not being up to the job, but isn't specific as to how improvements could be made;
- overlook or ignore ideas and contributions;
- ask the employee to produce time-consuming pieces of work, but never gives feedback or recognition, or takes the credit for it;
- 'forget' to warn the employee about meetings in time so there is no time to prepare;
- be openly aggressive, or make inappropriate remarks about gender, race, sexual orientation or beliefs;
- touch an employee inappropriately or sexually harass him or her;
- threaten redundancy or dismissal;
- make it difficult for an employee to take time off work;

- treat an employee more harshly than other colleagues;
- pick on an employee for no reason or humiliate them in public.

These are just a very few of the ways a bully may operate. What can be done if someone you know is being bullied at work and is feeling depressed as a result? You might:

- remind them that bullies often act in the way they do because they are trying to hide their own inadequacy – it will help them to recognize this and be aware that the bully has a problem;
- advise them to keep a diary of everything that happens – the pattern, quantity and regularity of incidents;
- discuss with them how they might tackle the bully about their behaviour;
- suggest they take the matter up with their union representative if they have one, or personnel department. The company they work for may have an anti-bullying, harassment or general grievance policy.

Retirement

It is easy to underestimate the impact retirement may have. Work is often central to our lives and our sense of self-esteem and pride, so it means more than merely providing an income. It can give a sense of purpose, social network and status too. The transition from work to retirement amounts to a loss and it is not uncommon to experience a range of emotions – from feeling numb, to sad or depressed. So even if someone knows that the day is looming when they have to retire and has plenty of time to prepare for it, they may still find the transition very difficult. If retirement is forced upon them, perhaps because effectively they have been made redundant, then it can be even more difficult to manage.

Retirement can have an effect on someone's confidence levels, their sense of self-worth and also on their relationships. Even if the person and their partner has been looking forward to retirement, finding that you then have to spend all day together can take its toll – if a man retires and his partner has been used to being at home alone, then in a sense the man is invading her territory. Boundaries may be crossed, and tempers may flare. If money is a problem, then choices may seem limited and it takes a lot of energy and commitment to fill your day if you can't afford to do the things you would really like to do. Boredom is the enemy – lots of time with not enough to do may give the person too much opportunity to feel fed up, become negative, and sink into a depression.

Tackling retirement

Preparing well for retirement is one of the best ways of ensuring it becomes a positive transition – thinking about the pros and the cons, making plans about how to spend one's time, deciding on new goals, and having a positive attitude will all help. Finding things to do that will maintain interests, create new ones, and ensure the time is fulfilling are all key. And talking about feelings is important too.

Moving house

We all regularly read that moving house is stressful, but it is quite hard to understand this unless you have been through the experience yourself. It can be stressful even if it's an experience someone is looking forward to. Why is it so stressful? There are many possible reasons: the strain of having strangers tramp around your home and wondering if they'll put in an offer; dealing with estate agents; trying to find somewhere new to buy or rent; trying to raise the finance; dealing with solicitors; trying to dovetail a sale and purchase; packing up possessions; and perhaps having to sell or give some away in order to fit into a smaller home; the need to put possessions into 'storage' while trying to find a new home; dealing with removal firms; settling into somewhere new with all that that entails – from making new friends, to finding one's way around a new area, settling children into school, coping with things that didn't live up to expectation after moving in, and so on.

If a move is forced on someone for any reason – because they have financial difficulties or have to move for work reasons – then the strain may be even greater.

Exams

Most people would say that they find taking exams stressful, but for some the worry and fear of failing – or actually failing – may be a significant contributory factor in a depressive episode. Many young people feel under tremendous pressure to achieve particular grades to get a college or university place; some worry about letting their parents down, or are put under constant pressure from parents to do well. If you come from a family where exam success is deemed important, it can be very stressful if you find you are not doing as well as you hoped. If you have an older brother or sister who has already set a high standard, then you may be worried you won't live up to that and feel afraid you will be judged a failure by comparison.

Some young people may be good academically and do well in 'course work', but find exams very difficult. The pressure may mean that some simply do not retain as much information when revising as others, while some young people 'fall apart' in the exam room, unable to remember anything they have revised.

What you can do if you are a parent

If you are a parent, it's very hard to strike a balance between encouraging your son or daughter and putting them under too much pressure. After all, you want them to do well and you want them to know that you are supporting them. Telling them you will love them regardless of how well they do in their exams will, of course, help, but unless this a message they consistently hear from a young age, the reality may be that they still feel under enormous pressure. Even if you do and say all the right things, they may still feel under pressure because of their own high standards or low self-esteem. The worry is that they will hide how bad they are really feeling inside because they don't want to admit to how worried they are and they don't want to be a disappointment. There are no easy answers – if you wait until the exams are imminent and then try to tell them that you don't mind if they fail, it may be a question of too little, too late. These ideas may help:

56

- Do your best to keep a dialogue open and encourage them to talk to you about their feelings.
- Encouraging them to 'be positive' is always a good idea, but it will help reduce pressure if you both talk about what might go wrong and have a 'Plan B' if they fail their exams. Discussing the possibility of failure and the course of action that would be taken if that happened won't make failure an inevitability – on the contrary, it may give your son or daughter a kind of 'safety valve' so they can relax into the revision without the pressure of thinking that it will be the end of the world if they fail.
- Help as far as you feel able from a practical point of view by a bit of extra pampering during tough revision periods – plentiful supplies of nutritious food, hot drinks, etc.
- Encourage your son or daughter to take regular exercise – why not go for a walk or a run together or encourage them to have a game of squash, or whatever happens to be their interest? Exercise will help keep their spirits and energy levels up.

Financial problems

Most people worry about money sometimes, but serious financial problems can trigger depression in some people. Relate, the relationship experts, say that money still ranks as the number one point of conflict in a relationship.

Many people are embarrassed to admit they are 'no good' with money and hide financial problems until it feels as though it is too late to do anything about them.

Dealing with money worries

If you think your partner is worried about money, then talking things through before it gets to the point where he or she feels the situation has become out of control will obviously help. But if money is not a subject you normally discuss together – and many couples do not – then it won't be easy.

If someone cannot pay a bill, then the worst thing they can do is to ignore it and hope it will go away. It is vital to contact the utility company/mortgage company, explain the difficulty, and try to come to a mutually agreed solution. If meeting the mortgage payment is a problem, again it is vital not to ignore the situation. The mortgage lender may, for example, be willing to accept a nominal payment for a limited period of time, or it may be possible to switch to an interest-only repayment plan which could be considerably cheaper, or extend the loan so that it can be paid back over a longer period. The National Debtline and your local Citizens Advice Bureau can offer guidance and ideas to help.

Unemployment

There is considerable evidence (Martin, 1997) that unemployment can have a detrimental effect on psychological as well as physical health. It is not just the strain of living on a reduced income – being unemployed can have a profound effect on someone's morale and feelings of self-worth. Society's expectations of men to be the 'breadwinner' can mean that men are even more vulnerable than women to depression as a consequence of unemployment. Many other factors feed into the link between depression and unemployment – for example, the resulting lack of control someone can feel in terms of their own destiny; the temptation for some to resort to drinking more alcohol to blot out the psychological pain or simply help pass the time – which in turn acts as a depressant; and the social isolation – if someone is unemployed, but most of their friends and family are working, they may feel cut off from others, and therefore feel cast adrift from their normal support network.

Losing a job – either because you are sacked or made redundant – brings its own pressures in terms of loss of self-esteem. For others, short-term contracts and the fear of losing a job can harm psychological health – especially if someone has a family to support; can't or doesn't want to move to a new area because of commitments or concerns about changing children's schools for instance; worries about loss of income, and so on. Again it is the loss of control over one's own destiny that takes a toll.

What you can do to help someone facing unemployment:

● It sounds simplistic, but talking, understanding, being sympathetic, giving the person a chance to talk about how they feel, voice their deepest fears, and even rant and rave if they need to, will all be of enormous value.

- If they are severely depressed, it may be a question of just being with them, showing you care, being there for them whenever you feel able.
- Talking through options may not be appropriate, depending on how severely depressed the person is. But having a goal to work towards could be a turning point. You may be able to help by finding out information, making suggestions, looking things up on the Internet, alerting them to possibilities they haven't thought of, and so on.
- Find ways to boost the person's self-esteem. They may not be working, but they do have skills they could utilize in other ways – whether it's decorating, doing voluntary work, taking a role in a local group or society, helping others, etc. Obviously you can't *make* them do anything – and they may be too ill to contemplate any of these ideas – but if you can be a small part of helping keep their mind open to the possibilities and opportunities, you will be offering support.

Holidays

It may seem strange, but particular occasions such as holidays fill some people with dread – Christmas, New Year, Thanksgiving, annual summer holidays, and birthdays, etc. The demands of all the extra pressures of these times – whether it's coping with family and friends; finding the money to pay for presents or extra food; the built-in expectation that these are occasions that must be enjoyed, and all the inherent stress and worries involved in making it an enjoyable time for others in the family; even the break in routine and the extra food and alcohol that is likely to be consumed; and, for some, a post-holiday anti-climax feeling – these are all factors that can pile on the stress and may pre-empt depression. Therefore it is a good idea to plan ahead for these occasions and offer extra support.

6

But how do *you* feel?

Seeing depression at close hand can be heartbreaking, especially if you feel there is little you can do to help. But if you are the wife, husband, partner, parent, child, brother, sister or friend of someone who is depressed, there may be things you can do to help. But you also have to look after yourself too.

Living with someone who is preoccupied by negative thoughts, unable to make decisions, or feels permanently hopeless about their future can be incredibly upsetting and frustrating. It may seem that no matter how much effort you are prepared to put in by trying to say just the 'right' thing, or showing how much you sympathize or care, at the end of the day it doesn't seem to make a difference. There will probably be times when it will seem as though the person who is depressed is 'doing it on purpose', as it can seem impossible that all your efforts are still not enough. It can be so hard to stand back and remind yourself that he or she is ill. It can seem even worse if on the outside the person has everything to live for: if they have no money worries; a nice home; a lovely family; a good job; supportive friends ... and you. It may seem incomprehensible that they are suffering from depression. Your perception might be that your own lot is worse than theirs, yet you are managing to cope.

If the person you love has manic depression it can seem like a roller-coaster ride that you may not be able to keep up with or fathom. The moment you get the measure of what is going on and what the person is going through, the ground can appear to shift, and once again there is a colossal swing back to a diametrically opposed mood – and it seems as if you are meant to take it all in your stride and not over-react; in other words, cope with whatever is thrown at you. When the person who has manic depression is on a high, you don't know whether to be pleased or fearful. And when everything simmers down and they become depressed again, you can find yourself feeling guilty at the sheer relief that they are no longer on a high, yet feeling desperately sorry for them that they are feeling so low again. Not only are you having to contend with their roller-coaster of emotion and mood swings, but you inevitably have to ride a roller-coaster of your own emotions too.

On top of all this you have the everyday realities of depression to cope with: seeing the person you love deteriorate, or seemingly become 'another' person before your eyes, plus having to cope with a range of symptoms that affect every moment of every day. And if *you* are finding it hard to cope, you may wonder who you can turn to – it can feel selfish to complain or be concerned about your own sadness, anger, impatience and worry when it is not you who is supposed to be ill.

For many it is the loss of the relationship they once had that is so hard to bear: disappointment and sadness that the person you love is not the person you married, or is not the same old mum or dad, or the friend you used to have. If the person has changed and your relationship has changed too, you may feel unbearably sad – coming to terms with it may be extremely hard to do.

Of course, this is the bleakest picture and it isn't always as bleak as this. Some people live with someone who is depressed for years, become accustomed to the illness, and cope well. For others it is a different story. It is important to stress that no two people's depression is the same and everyone copes differently.

You might imagine that someone who is depressed would welcome companionship, yet what they may crave more is time alone. It very much depends on their personal circumstances and the events that may have led to the depression, but if they are feeling very stressed, and struggling with a range of responsibilities, and roles they need to juggle – as a wife, mother, career woman, for example – the chance to have 'time out' and replenish their batteries could really help. If your efforts to offer consolation, sympathy and advice are rejected, it may simply be that they are too tired and exhausted to listen, however well-intentioned your motives, because they have no 'mental space' left over to respond. If you are in a position to help give them practical support and enable them to take a break away from pressing responsibilities, then this could be of enormous value.

If the person you love is sometimes or often angry, you may wonder if they can be depressed in the first place. Yet irritability and anger may be a symptom of depression in some people, while others feel angry and are unable to express it. Anger may result from a long-standing inability to express feelings and emotions, feeling that others have taken advantage or have treated them unfairly – and anger can, of course, be a perfectly normal reaction in many situations! If you are able to recognize these feelings it may help, especially as their anger, although seemingly directed at you, may actually be about someone else or another issue entirely. So try not to take it personally. Also, look for the sense in what they are saying. Their anger may be scary to deal with, but if you can see why they are angry and sympathize, and show them you agree that they have a right to be angry, then you may be able to help take the heat out of the situation; it may be a much better approach than trying to 'talk them out' of being angry.

Caring for or living with someone who has depression can be hard if that person does not respond in the way you expect. If they are not grateful or appreciative or willing to be looked after or take your advice – not necessarily because they have depression but just because everyone is an individual and has a different personality – then it can seem an uphill struggle. But the illness of depression inevitably has an effect on some aspects of how some people are able to respond and communicate. You may be trying your hardest to do everything you can to help, but they may ignore you, reject your help, be angry, or even refuse to speak to you. All you can do is whatever you feel you can do, no more and no less.

You may have to adjust to your changing role too. If the person you love is experiencing a major depressive episode, then you may have become a carer too.

You may wonder if you should tell your friends and family that someone close to you has depression, especially if you believe that it may change how they view that person or how they view you. If coming to terms with depression has been hard for you, it may also be hard for others. You may find that some of those you thought would rally round behave in an unexpected way, shunning you or avoiding the subject altogether. This is unlikely to be a deliberate strategy to hurt you – but simply because they don't know how to handle their own reactions. They may be frightened of depression, they may not really understand what it is. Or they may not know what to say, how to be, what to do.

Bear in mind that someone who is cold and rejecting of you or the person who has depression may feel in turmoil on the inside, at a complete loss to know what to say to you. It may seem ironic, but you may need to reach out and help them – to break the ice and show them you realize it is hard for them too.

You may feel that you somehow don't have the right to talk about your feelings – after all, if you're not the person who is depressed, you may feel your needs are not as great as theirs. But you count too. And sometimes it's important to have someone listen to your problems, however trivial they may seem in comparison.

Case history: Linda
My partner has had depression on and off for more than seven years, and I have found it very helpful to join a self-help group in my area for carers. Although I don't have to care for all my partner's physical needs, my life is restricted in many ways. Friends are no longer interested in coming to the house and I don't like to leave Terry for long. He has been suicidal many times, and he doesn't always remember to take his medication.

I have a part-time job as a dinner lady and that keeps me going – being with children who are usually happy and smiling is a great antidote to being with someone who is depressed. I know he can't help it, but there are times when I get very angry with him and then feel very guilty. Yes, it is an illness, but there are still times when I think he could make more effort and that he uses the illness because he is lazy. But that sounds like such a terrible thing to say that I don't dare say it to anyone in the family or anyone we know. Before all this, we had a good relationship. We used to enjoy dancing, going on holiday, and doing lots of ordinary things together. Now we are stuck at home and it's like living with a stranger sometimes. He is not the man I married and sometimes I cry at night thinking that I'll never get that man back again. I try to stay optimistic, but it's very hard. My own health has suffered. I suffer from anxiety and my weight has dropped.

Even our grown-up children aren't keen to come home any more, so I don't get to see our grandchildren as often as I would like to. They don't understand his illness, they just see him sitting there unable to have a conversation half the time and never interested in what they are doing or what the grandchildren are doing – no wonder they don't want to come.

It's Christmas I dread most. We never get invited anywhere any more and the kids don't want to come to us. So we sit in here, watching telly all day, wearing our party hats and feeling as miserable as sin. To me, Terry's depression seems like a life sentence, not just for him – but for me too. The doctors say there is no reason why he won't get better, but I worry he will never be the same old Terry. I just want it all to go away and be happy again.

When you live with someone who has depression, your role and relationship with that person may change whether you like it or not. Partners may feel cast in the role of mother or carer – and it will take time to adjust, sort out how you feel, and how you can best help and cope.

No matter how much you care for or love someone who is depressed, you can't make them better – and that can be so frustrating. You may feel resentful, angry, helpless, sad both for yourself and the other person – a torrent of conflicting emotions. One minute you may feel positive, the next very negative. Or perhaps you don't know how you feel.

Try answering the following questions – you may find some of them very hard, but try to be honest:

- Do you feel the person you love has changed since becoming depressed?
- Do you feel you have changed?
- How did you feel when they first began to experience depression?
- How do you feel now?
- Do you find it harder now to be sympathetic?
- Have you made changes to your own social life so you can cope with their depression?
- Are you finding it more difficult to work as a result of their depression – or have you had to give up work?
- Do you feel you have anyone to talk to about how you feel?
- Has the depression adversely affected your relationship with them?
- Do you sometimes feel you don't know how to help or what to say?

- Are you feeling anxious?
- Are you lonely?
- Are you upset most days?
- Do you worry that somehow their depression is your fault?
- Do you feel angry with them?
- Have friends and family commented that they are worried about you?
- Do you worry that you are neglecting friends and family or work because of the person's depression?
- Do you feel your life revolves around their life?
- Are you able to 'switch off' from their depression and regularly have time to yourself?
- Are you able to enjoy yourself when you are away from them?
- Are you worried about the future?
- Are you concerned that you may become depressed?

You will know yourself from your answers to these questions just how far your loved one's depression is impacting on your own life – and your own well-being. To repeat: you are important too. No matter how strong you think you are, it is vital to care for yourself – even more so if the person you love relies on you and you want to be there for them.

Learning to deal with emotions is hard. There are bound to be days when you feel ground down and everything seems bleak. There are no easy answers, but the following may help:

- Try not to look too far into the future – make a point of gaining as much joy as you can out of every single day. Don't put off your life until the person you love is better – live for each moment if you can.
- Don't waste time dwelling on regrets – it won't change a thing. You are not to blame for someone else's illness, and you could not have prevented it by anything you did or didn't do. Concentrate on how you can enjoy life more despite the restrictions and negative aspects.
- Don't allow negative thoughts to fester – push them away and don't allow them to take over.
- Accept how you feel – there are no rights and wrongs. Don't make yourself feel worse because you think you shouldn't feel angry or shouldn't feel sad.

- Try writing down what you feel. You may be able to express in writing what you can't say in words. Keeping a diary may be a lifeline – remember to write in what happened on the good days as well as the bad days, as looking back and seeing there were good times too can be useful.
- If you don't feel like writing, then try expressing yourself in some other way – painting a picture, for instance. You don't need to be 'good at art' – just experiment with colour and shapes and see what happens.
- Try to find a safe place to express your emotions – a friend or family member, or even a counsellor if you think you would find it useful.
- Don't constantly check your emotions – when you feel like having a good cry, then try not to hold it in.
- If you have the chance to join a support group, then consider it. Talking to other people who are going through a similar experience could be very beneficial.
- Try not to dwell on what you might have done, 'should' have done, or didn't do. Accept that no one is perfect and you are doing the best you can most of the time. Accept and learn from any mistakes you have made.
- By the same token, give yourself permission not to be 'perfect' all the time. Accept yourself for who you are, imperfections included! No one gets it right all the time.
- Be aware of your fears – fear that things will never get back to normal, that you too may become depressed, or concerns about suicide. These fears are common. Confront your fears – but don't let them dominate your life.

One problem you may experience is discovering that you actually find it easier to live with the depressed person when he or she is depressed. This may sound ridiculous, but can present quite a challenge and may even cause you to feel guilty. Psychiatrist Anthony Clare, in the book he jointly wrote with Spike Milligan (*Depression and How to Survive It* – see Further Reading), gives a good example: someone who is normally over-critical, over-demanding, very assertive, vain and inconsiderate may well become quieter, less demanding and so on when depressed – and easier to live with. If you recognize this scenario, you may feel guilty that you enjoy the depressive phase because it gives you some respite. Acknowledge to yourself that you feel this way – it is a perfectly understandable feeling and there is no need to feel guilty about it.

You may have to come to terms with the fact that life may never be the same again. It is tempting to look back to how things used to be when the person you love was well, when you could do what you wanted, when you wanted. But now perhaps your commitments are different. Changes that are forced upon us can be much more difficult to cope with.

Learning to live in the present isn't easy – but can make a big difference to how well you cope. So how can you look after *you* as well as being concerned for, or caring for, the person you love who has depression?

More ideas

- Even if you feel you have to put all your energy into caring for someone who has depression, it is so very important to ensure you have time for yourself too.
- Redefine your priorities. What is important to you now? It is not selfish to think of yourself too. It might mean spending more time, effort and resources on eating a better diet, taking regular exercise, or treating yourself once in a while.
- Set realistic goals. This will give you something to work towards, targets to aim for, and achievements to look back on and be proud of. In future years you will be glad you have other things you can look back on and be happy about.
- Accept your limitations. Give others in the family the chance to take on more responsibility – they might enjoy it.
- Learn how to say no – spending time with people you don't like, or attending functions you don't want to attend, will sap precious energy you might want to save.

How to deal with negative thoughts

- If you are finding it particularly hard to cope, allow yourself a 'worry' ten minutes every day. This is the time you can really let rip with all your frustrations, anger and other negative emotions.

Or write down how you feel. Then STOP! Get into the habit of saving up the worst of how you feel for a short concentrated period of time rather than sliding into the habit of feeling discontented and worried throughout the day.

- If you tend to lie in bed at night worrying, or suffer sleepless nights when you toss and turn with endless thoughts running through your mind, make a list of exactly what you are worried about and resolve to deal with these things in the morning. The sheer act of writing out a list is a mysterious process, and a positive step that can help you to put worries to one side and allow you to have a better night's sleep. Another trick is to have a 'worry' side and a 'non-worry' side. Lie on your 'worry side' for the first ten minutes when getting into bed and let all the troubles you are feeling have their say. Then turn onto your 'non-worry' side and refuse to let them in. The simple physical action of turning over is like turning your back on your worries. Be determined that you will never worry on your 'non-worry' side! It sounds daft, but can be surprisingly effective.
- Try not to 'catastrophize' – assume the worst about everything. It can make you feel far more hopeless and helpless than necessary.
- Don't waste time thinking of regrets – it won't change a thing. Concentrate your energy on how you can make the best of things, despite the setbacks.

Getting a good night's sleep

Not getting enough sleep or finding that your sleep pattern is disturbed is a common symptom of depression – and if you are caring for someone who has depression it may apply to you as well. Worrying about not getting enough sleep can make the problem worse, leading to a vicious circle. The following tips may help:

- Get up at the same time each day, whether you are sleepy or not.
- Only go to bed when you are tired.
- If you wake during the night, don't worry that you are 'losing' sleep; instead of tossing and turning, get up and do something

BUT HOW DO *YOU* FEEL?

mundane – reading, a jigsaw, knitting, listening to quiet music –
until you feel sleepy again.

- If waking early is a problem, again the best advice is to get up
rather than toss and turn.
- Avoid watching television or reading anything too stimulating
before trying to sleep.
- Ensure the bedroom is dark, quiet and well ventilated.
- The ideal temperature for a bedroom is cool – below 70°F
(21°C) is ideal.
- Avoid any kind of stimulants for at least $1\frac{1}{2}$ hours before bedtime
– so no tea, coffee, cola drinks, cocoa, hot chocolate or alcohol.
- Don't smoke just before bedtime as nicotine is a stimulant too.
- Avoid eating too late in the evening.
- Have a milky drink about half-an-hour before bed – but not if
getting up in the night to go to the toilet is likely to be a
problem.
- Try hard to take some exercise during the day to help tire you
out physically.

Reducing stress

When the body is under stress, the brain activates the autonomic
nervous system in a bid to help us cope – the 'fight or flight'
response we mentioned earlier in the book. This primitive response
involves the release of adrenaline, which stimulates the delivery of
oxygen to the brain and muscles, preparing them for action by
increasing the heart and breathing rate (which would help you run
away or fight if faced with danger). In addition, the adrenal glands
are stimulated to release a hormone called cortisol, which raises the
blood pressure. But if adrenaline and cortisol are released and not
'used up', and instead of fighting or running away all these actions
take place in the body when you are sedentary – as so often
happens if you get stressed – then unpleasant symptoms result: the
classic signs of stress. Symptoms include chest pain, diarrhoea,
headaches, tiredness, changes to the appetite, dry mouth, inability
to concentrate, poor memory, palpitations and generally feeling
agitated or unwell.

It is thought that if your body is regularly primed for action but you remain sedentary, then the adrenaline and cortisol released depress the immune system, making you more susceptible to infections and inclined to feel run down. In addition, if adrenaline and cortisol are secreted into the bloodstream in large amounts, they cause fatty acids to be released into the blood from stores in the body. A persistent elevation of fatty acid blood levels can impair the circulation, and in the long run may put you at a greater risk of a heart attack.

Stress-reducing and relaxation techniques can help reduce the heart rate and lower high blood pressure. Even very simple stress-relieving techniques will help, such as:

- Take some deep breaths – breathe in through the nostrils, to the count of five, hold for two seconds, and breathe out to the count of five.
- Create some peace and quiet for yourself – go for a walk, read a book, listen to some calming music.
- Close your eyes and visualize a calming scene, such as walking by a stream on a summer's day.
- Have a good stretch – raise your arms and feel the stretch in your body from your fingertips to your toes.

7

How to help someone who is depressed

The very nature of depression means that someone who is depressed tends to withdraw from family and friends at the very time they most need your love, support and understanding.

It can be extremely hard to imagine what they are going through, especially if they seem withdrawn, cold and distant on the outside. Be aware that though they may seem 'cut off' from you, the chances are they feel in turmoil on the inside, afraid, bursting with emotion or, conversely, completely numb, gripped by sadness and fear, and at a loss to know what to say to you. They may well be feeling it is their fault they are ill and unable to cope, sad at the burden they may feel to you, and uncertain about the kind of future they face. Perhaps they feel angry that it happened to them; or angry with other people who do not seem to understand what they are going through; disappointed at how their body and mind has let them down; and upset that certain hopes and dreams now seem unobtainable; guilt about not being able to fulfil responsibilities as a wife, mother, father, son, daughter or friend, or because they know they are often demanding or feel they don't deserve all the understanding you show; fearful about what the future holds, and whether they will ever get better.

At this time you may need to reach out and help them, show them you care. Even saying things that seem ludicrously simple like 'It's all right. I know this is difficult for you. And it is difficult for me. But I want to be with you, I want to be here for you' can help to break the ice. This may not be easy if you are struggling to come to terms with your own feelings and emotions, but if you can keep open the communication lines at this point it will help you both.

Also, showing you understand that depression is an illness – that you know the person is not simply being weak or a wimp, or difficult or attention-seeking. Letting them know that you recognize it as an illness will almost certainly offer huge relief. And if you are able to offer your support – whether it is a sympathetic ear, unconditional love, practical help or simply letting them know you are 'there' for them – then you really could make a difference. Remember someone who is depressed already feels bad about themselves and may also blame themselves for their illness and for the worry they are putting loved ones through. You may be able to do a lot to help and your suggestions and ideas may be valid and useful, but a sympathetic, caring approach will be appreciated.

In what other ways might you help? The following ideas may help, but may be inappropriate for a variety of reasons – perhaps because the person you love who has depression is simply too ill to respond to some of these, because you are not in a position to try the ideas suggested, or because they just don't seem appropriate in your individual circumstances. There is a danger that some suggestions may seem patronizing – either because they are totally inappropriate in your case, because they seem too basic, or for some other reason. That's fine. What suits one person may not suit another. But I hope there is at least something in this chapter that might be of use or give food for thought:

- Listen sympathetically. This may sound easy, but even if you consider yourself a 'good listener', one problem is that someone who is depressed isn't always able to articulate their feelings – quite often they won't feel like speaking at all, and may just sit there. Even if you try to coax them and let them know you want to listen, they may still be unable to open up. In this situation, you can be of enormous help simply by sitting with them, or holding their hand if appropriate. Try to get a sense of whether it might even be better not to try to get them to talk at all if it is too painful for them, but to accept the silence instead, freeing them of the pressure to speak. This in itself is a loving act, and though they may not be able to express how they feel, they will still appreciate your sensitivity to their feelings.
- If they are able to open up, resist the temptation to jump in almost before they have finished speaking to give advice – let them set the pace. They may need to tell you all their thoughts and feelings in detail – and however much you think you know what is going on for them, or that you know what is 'best' for them, it is only by listening carefully that you will have any chance of really understanding. Often it is the little details that are so important – they may need to tell you all their thoughts

72

and feelings in minutiae; see your role as a good listener rather than as an opportunity for you to tell them what to do. That is not to say you can never offer advice or suggestions, but don't make the mistake of rushing in too soon. You may have the most wonderful opportunity to be literally the only person who is willing to really listen, and hear and understand what they are trying to say and give it due consideration, thought and appreciation before appearing to rush in with 'off the top of the head' ideas and suggestions.

- Don't say: 'I know just how you feel' even if you think you do. And avoid constantly trying to chip in with examples of 'similar' things you think have happened to you that have made you feel the 'same' way. Make the most of the opportunity to hear their story, not tell yours. The danger is that if what you say doesn't resonate with them or they simply aren't well enough to listen to your story, they will switch off and you will have lost a golden opportunity to listen.

- Be affectionate. You can show your care, concern and love in so many ways. How you show affection will depend on the relationship you have with the depressed person – terms of endearment, reminding them you love them no matter what, leaving them an affectionate note to find, bringing them a cup of tea in bed. All these little gestures can mean such a tremendous amount.

- Touch is a powerful way of showing you care – a hand on the shoulder, holding hands, a hug, a foot or head massage, stroking their hand; this will, of course, depend on the relationship you have with the person.

- Spend time with them. We all lead such frenetic lives most of the time and there is always so much to do, and a pressure to be somewhere doing something, that it can be incredibly hard just to do nothing. But sitting and spending time with someone who is depressed, even if you do nothing but sit together, can be incredibly valuable and really helps to show your support. Sometimes depression can be so severe that the person cannot face doing ordinary things we all take for granted – such as reading a newspaper or watching a television programme; if this is the case, then it will be hard just to sit and do nothing – but is still worthwhile. Just being there for them, without pressure, no

73

coaxing to do this or that, an acceptance of the fact that they can't face doing anything at all, is what will really help.

- Talk if that's what they would like to do. It may be that the person wants to talk about their situation, and you can help by encouraging them to talk about their feelings. It's tempting to reel off a list of what you think they should or shouldn't do, or suggestions as to how they might make changes in their life – but let them set the pace. If you bombard them with your opinions and ideas it will be more difficult for them to find their own way. Make suggestions if you feel they are appropriate, but listening carefully is important too. It's difficult because if you are too opinionated and aggressive in your response, the person may clam up altogether. The art is to listen, and to encourage the person to come up with their own solutions.

  Be aware they may be worrying about being a burden to you and may conceal how they really feel because they do not want to be a worry to you. Be honest, tell them you are worried, but perhaps that you will worry more if they close off from you.

- Help them formulate goals. Whether it's something simple like going for a walk every day or something more ambitious such as taking up a new interest, your input may help.

- Help to increase the number of positive things that happen in their life. You can't wave a magic wand, and you can only do what you can do; but if you are able to help increase the number of positive things in their life, it could be of enormous value. What you can do will depend on your relationship with the person who is depressed, and the amount of time etc. you have. But it could be something as simple as asking them over for a coffee, or turning up on their doorstep with a flask of hot chocolate and a large cream cake! It might be going for a walk in the park, encouraging them to join a self-help group, or planning a holiday.

- Suggest that increasing routine tasks may be a good idea – there is a prevailing attitude in society that 'routine' is dull, but having a routine can give shape to the day if you are ill or just going through a bad patch. It can feel reassuring to have a routine during difficult times – whether it's walking the dog at the same time each day, or even something as banal as having a cup of tea and a biscuit at 11 a.m. and turning on the television to watch a particular programme at the same time every day. Adding on 'new' routines can be helpful and give more meaning to the day too.

- Have a good laugh with them – just because someone is depressed doesn't mean you can't have a smile if the opportunity presents itself. Watching a funny video together could be a good way of switching off from troubles.

- Encourage them to keep a diary. For some, the act of writing down thoughts gives a kind of 'release', a way of organizing thoughts, getting rid of anger, expressing difficult or worrying thoughts they may not be able to express verbally even to you, and possibly also a chance to notice recurring themes – negative thinking patterns, for example.

- Help them to think of areas in their life that are positive – it is easy to lose sight of the things we value when we feel down.

- Remember to encourage and praise when appropriate; this may sound patronizing, but it needn't be – we can all do with a bit of praise and encouragement! But this will help to keep up morale and may build self-esteem – so long as what you say is genuine.

- Encourage them to eat a balanced diet. Some people who are depressed eat too much or resort to eating junk food simply because they can't be bothered to cook for themselves or make an effort to eat healthily. Others may just not feel like bothering to eat or may even forget to eat. But a poor diet means a low intake of essential vitamins and minerals, so anything you can do with regard to this matter will help make a difference. (You can read more about diet in Chapter 11.)

- Don't try to 'chivvy' them out of it. Depression is an illness, and though giving your support and encouragement is valuable, you can't speed up the course of the illness by being overly positive or trying to compensate for their negativity.

- Don't try to force them to engage in social activities if they don't want to. On the other hand, research shows that good, close social support can be a key factor in protecting someone from depression and in recovery from depression; so if you can help keep lines of support open with regard to close family and friends, it could be of enormous help. This may mean talking about the person's depression to help others understand. This is difficult because it is very important to observe confidentiality and not break trust, but if you are able to sensitively raise the topic of depression in a general way with friends and family without breaking trust, and without talking about the person concerned in their absence, you may be able to explain that depression is an illness, what the symptoms are, how it manifests itself, and how others may be able to help.

• If your partner is depressed and you have always done things together, you may now need to 'redraw' social lines and build up some sort of social life independently if you can no longer do things as a couple.

• Learn as much as you can about depression and treatments so you are knowledgeable. This will give you a better chance to help, although ultimately the person who is depressed will have to take responsibility for their own illness and treatment. It will, of course, help if the person you love finds out more about their own depression. This can give the person with depression some sense of control over their illness – a feeling of empowerment is especially important as depression so often makes people feel powerless and out of control of their own lives. Knowing more about their illness can also help them to ask the right questions of doctors, so they are more informed and can make better decisions about treatments. At a simple level, learning more about depression can also dispel some of the myths that even people suffering from the illness may have – helping to reduce worries about 'going mad', for example.

• Don't forget about practical support too – it can be hard for someone who is depressed to summon up enough energy to remember to pay the bills, get the shopping, clean the house, etc., so anything you can do to help is likely to be valuable and a practical way of showing you care.

• Find out what support is available in your local area in the way of services, self-help groups, etc.: talking to or keeping in touch with others who have depression – sharing experiences and information, talking about feelings – can be a lifeline for some. Some people who have depression find that joining a self-help group, such as those organized by the Depression Alliance, is very valuable because of the supportive, non-judgemental atmosphere they find.

• Several studies have suggested that writing poetry may help

76

someone recover from bereavement and depression. In one study carried out at the Bristol Royal Infirmary, 8 per cent of patients were able to come off antidepressants while attending a poetry rehabilitation programme. It seems as if there is something potentially very beneficial about having the opportunity to express your feelings in the written word. You don't need to be 'a writer' to enjoy writing poetry. Poems don't have to rhyme either! There is now a group called Survivors' Poetry, which was started by Hilary Porter. There are 30 groups throughout the UK and the charity offers poetry-writing workshops (see Useful Addresses).

As I have already said, some of these ideas may sound trite, so you must be guided by what seems appropriate in your individual circumstances – something that has real meaning for you and the person you love.

Challenging negative thinking

It may be appropriate to gently challenge negative thought patterns. If the person who has depression says 'everything always goes wrong for me', for example, you might gently question the 'always' and help them to think of times when things have gone right.

It is important to note that it is not only people who have depression who think negatively! And some of the ideas in this section may apply more to you, not the person who is depressed, or they may not be relevant at all. But other negative thought patterns include:

- Jumping to negative conclusions – making incorrect assumptions about other people's motives or about how other people think or regard them; or presuming negative things will happen, but without having any evidence for such assumptions.
- Discounting the positive – focusing only on the negative and completely ignoring the positive things that someone has said or the positive things that have happened.
- 'Catastrophizing' – when someone feels 'everything' has gone

wrong after they have made just one mistake; assuming the worst; or blowing out of all proportion mishaps or setbacks.

- Unrealistic expectations about themselves or others – feeling they should have been a better person, should or should not have done something they regard as important.
- Dwelling on mistakes.

So how can you counteract or challenge negative thinking? What kinds of things could you actually say? To express the following ideas to the person who has depression (or even to yourself!) might help:

- If you weren't depressed, do you think you would still think the same or would you view it differently?
- What is the evidence for you thinking that? Is it really true?
- Are there alternative explanations for that?
- What is the effect of thinking negatively, on you and on others?
- What would you need to do to see it in a more positive light?
- What would be the advantage of seeing it in a more positive light?
- How might you feel differently for instance?

Other possible ways to respond to negative statements are:

- You might say 'you could be right', but then gently change the subject. This may help take the heat out of the situation until you have the chance to discuss it more fully.
- You might value any good points made, including the negative ones – it's important not to assume that just because a point is negative it has no value. One advantage of being negative is that it enables a person to see potential problems and pitfalls that others may not see! So show the person you can see their negativity in a positive light.
- You might ask them to come up with a positive point for every negative point made.

These are just ideas and may not be appropriate – you are not trying to be a counsellor! Be guided by your relationship with the person and your own sense of what feels helpful. Trying to change the way we think is hard even when not depressed, but much more difficult for someone who is depressed.

Checklist for negative thinking

If someone is aware they are thinking negatively and wishes they could have a more positive approach, the following checklist may help them to review their way of looking at things and see alternative ways of thinking about a person or situation:

- Am I jumping to conclusions about this person or situation?
- Can I think of an alternative or more positive explanation?
- Am I taking an 'all or nothing' or 'black or white' stance on this person/issue? Is there an in-between view that might be a more reasonable explanation or interpretation?
- When I take an all or nothing stance, what's in it for me? What would I lose and gain by being more flexible in my approach?
- Am I catastrophizing about something that is not all that important in the great scheme of things and making myself miserable in the process?
- Am I focusing on my own weaknesses and shortcomings instead of my strengths?
- Am I writing myself off as a failure or unlovable just because I have made mistakes?
- Do I expect other people to be perfect? If not, and I accept that other people can make mistakes, then can I allow myself to make mistakes too?
- Am I blaming myself for something that is not my fault, or for a situation where the blame should at least be shared? Or perhaps it's not anyone's fault?
- Am I beating myself up for not being perfect all the time?
- Could I be over-reacting on this occasion?
- Am I worrying too much about things I can't change?

Ultimately it is important to realize that someone who is depressed may already feel they have little control in their own life, and so your efforts to help them may be rejected as interfering and make them feel worse, not better. Only you can make a judgement as to whether any of the above ideas are appropriate in your individual circumstances; only you can assess what will work for you and the person you love.

It may be that if you are the husband, wife, partner or parent of someone who is depressed, and they believe that you are part of the problem, you may need to examine the relationship you have with that person – you might need to be willing to make changes. It is tempting to assume that if someone is depressed then the illness is entirely theirs. But it may benefit not just the person who is depressed, but also you, if you are willing to take a long hard look at the relationship and the changes or improvements that could be made. You might, for instance, consider going to Relate or family therapy together.

But whatever your good intentions, and however strong a person you are, there is no doubt that living with someone who is depressed can be a gruelling, frustrating and often unrewarding experience. Accept that your advice and help may not be wanted or appropriate, and they may be rejected – or even accepted, but without thanks. But this help *may* be welcomed too – and you may play a key role in supporting that person at a time when other people turn their backs.

Dealing with the medical profession

One way you can offer to help is to attend doctor or hospital appointments so you can listen to what the treatment options are and, if appropriate, ask questions on the person's behalf. It may be easier for you to think of the right questions to ask, listen carefully to what is said, and remember the information afterwards. Again, this is not meant to sound patronizing, and no one is suggesting that someone who is depressed cannot think for themselves or make their own decisions perfectly well, but many of the symptoms of depression – such as an inability to concentrate, forgetfulness, as well as indecisiveness – can make doctor and hospital appointments stressful and worrying.

You may be able to be seen as the person's formal 'advocate' if the person is agreeable, in which case the medical profession will talk directly to you. This would also give you the opportunity to help the person you love to sort out practical issues such as standing up for their rights or claiming benefits. For further information about advocacy, contact MIND (see Useful Addresses).

Even if no treatment 'options' are offered – in most cases the only option offered may be antidepressants – it might be useful to ask about different types of antidepressants, how they work, how quickly they might work, possible side-effects, and so on. It may be that you are close enough to the person to help them weigh up treatment options, assuming there is a choice. Given that one of the symptoms of depression can be difficulty in making decisions, it may be a real problem for the person you live with to decide what to do for the best, so helping them talk it through could be an enormous help.

8

The ultimate fear: suicide

According to the World Health Organization, around 15–20 per cent of all people who have depression complete suicide. In fact, suicide is a leading cause of death for young adults, and among the top three causes of death in young men and women aged 15–34. In men under 35, suicide is the most common cause of death. For every person who completes suicide, there may be 20 people who attempt to do so.

In the UK, the latest figures (from the Samaritans, January 2003, and relating to the year 2000) show that there is one suicide every 82 minutes in the UK and Republic of Ireland – and three-quarters of those are men. In England alone around 5,000 people kill themselves every year. Depression is the most common mental disorder leading to suicide – and research from the World Health Organization shows that excess alcohol and access to firearms are both linked to suicide. The Samaritans say that, in youth suicide, alcohol and drug abuse is a highly significant factor – both alcohol and drugs affect thinking and reasoning ability, and can also act as depressants. The Department of Health says that being male, living alone, and unemployment are all risk factors for suicide, as are alcohol/drug misuse and mental ill health.

Other contributory factors in suicide include:

- *Family history of suicide or mental distress.* According to MIND, some 11 per cent of people who complete suicide had a first-degree relative who had also done so.
- *Family background.* Research shows that young people who attempt suicide tend to grow up in families where there are more problems – for example, 'broken homes' as a result of divorce or death, or where unemployment, addiction to alcohol or drugs, or mental illness is present (Kienhorst, as cited in Samaritans statistics).
- *Physical and sexual abuse.* Young people who have been abused, or are currently being abused, either physically or sexually, may also be at higher risk of suicide.

- *Prison.* Young people under 21 who are in prison or on remand may also be at higher risk (HM Prison Service, as cited in Samaritans statistics).
- It is also widely believed that low levels of the serotonin metabolite, 5-hydroxyindoleacetic acid (5-hydroxytryptamine), is a factor in suicide. (SSRI and TCA drugs are used to raise levels of serotonin in people who are depressed. For more information about treatments, see Chapter 10.)

In general, suicide rates are falling, which is good news. But *suicide attempts* are increasing in some age groups, notably in males aged 15–24; and according to the Samaritans, deliberate self-harm is most common in young women aged 15–19. The most common trigger for attempted suicide in young people is relationship problems. One in five of those who attempt suicide have attempted suicide on a previous occasion.

One study cited by MIND estimates that up to 70 per cent of suicides are by people who were, or had been, depressed. Research suggests that suicide is related to feeling hopeless about one's situation.

The warning signs in suicide

It is important to say that suicide cannot always be prevented, and sometimes there are no warning signs at all. Even if a person feels depressed, this may not be obvious to those closest to them – and someone who is determined to end their life may also be determined not to give any clues about what they are about to do.

Sometimes the warning signs are there, but they can still be extremely hard to spot. For loved ones looking on, it can be so hard to know just how desperate a person is, particularly if they are not sharing their feelings or disguising them. Even if the person talks about suicide, it is easy to convince oneself that they don't really mean it, or that they would not go through with it.

In some cases the warning signs are the same as typical symptoms of depression itself – difficulties in sleeping or waking up early, feelings of failure, or low self-esteem. Someone who feels completely hopeless about their life and feels that everything is pointless and futile is likely to be at higher risk.

Some people are not necessarily suicidal, but deliberately self-harming by burning, cutting or scratching themselves. This may be perceived as a way of releasing tension, but is very hard indeed for others to understand. Like attempted suicide, self-harm should be taken seriously and treated sympathetically – it may seem to outsiders that it is attention-seeking, weakness or lack of self-control, but it is a symptom of genuine, often unbearable distress and emotional pain for the person concerned.

What if the person actually talks about suicide? A common myth is that someone who talks about it won't 'go through with it', but this is entirely incorrect. If someone talks about suicide, or threatens suicide, then it is a clear indication that they have considered suicide as an option, however briefly, and they should be taken seriously. This is difficult as some people can feel that when a loved one threatens suicide, particularly if it is something they do on a regular basis, that it is not because they seriously intend to take their own life, but simply as a way of gaining attention, controlling family members, or trying to get their own way on a particular issue. There are no easy answers, and you may feel you are in a much better position than an outsider to judge what the situation really is. But it is certainly the case, statistically, that 20 per cent of those who complete suicide have attempted suicide on a previous occasion. MIND says that most people who have taken their own lives did speak to someone about it beforehand. Certainly, if the person you love starts to say they no longer care about anything or 'you won't need to worry about me any more' or 'I won't be here anyway', or something similar, it's important to take it seriously. Even if suicide is not seriously being contemplated, these remarks highlight how desperate the person is feeling, and how in need of help and support they are.

You may feel sure that such remarks are more to do with trying to emotionally manipulate you – and once you begin to think like this it is very hard to switch off from that viewpoint, and it may become harder and harder for you to become objective. If this is the case, you might consider taking soundings from others in the family – has anyone else noticed a change in the person who is depressed? Have they been hinting at suicide to other people?

Another possible warning sign is a distinct or sudden change in behaviour: someone who is depressed who 'suddenly' seems to become more withdrawn, or eager to tell you that they now feel fine; someone who suddenly seems to be very calm and collected when hours before was very agitated, or vice versa; someone who has been talking to you about how they feel, but then suddenly doesn't want to talk at all; or someone who suddenly withdraws from all social contact and wants to shut themselves away. This kind of transformation in behaviour may be a sign that they have decided to attempt suicide.

Other more obvious clues may be a sudden decision to sort out their affairs; give away money or possessions; write letters to family members they haven't seen for some time, or significant family members they see regularly; visit places that were once important to them or significant in some way; as well as a sudden desire to make a will, or sort out details regarding their own funeral.

Ironically, there may be a higher risk of suicide when someone who has been suffering from depression seems to be feeling a bit better – it may be that all their renewed energy and enthusiasm is going into planning their own death.

But it is certainly a myth that people who talk about suicide never intend to kill themselves – or that someone who attempts suicide, and who does not then kill themselves for whatever reason, did not really mean to take their own life.

Can you prevent the suicide of someone you love?

It may be that you never notice the warning signs – or, sadly, there may be no warning signs to notice. If this is the case, there is little you can do. If someone you love has depression, you are probably already doing as much as you can to help. Talking to the person – and encouraging them to talk to you – is one of the best things you can possibly do to keep lines of communication open and help them feel they are not alone.

It may be that you see warning signs, but don't know how to help and feel powerless to intervene. Again, talking – and encouraging the person to talk to you – is vital. Even more important is trying to persuade them to seek help from their doctor. You may want to rally support from other friends and family. If you are very concerned and don't know what to do, then telephone the Samaritans for guidance or contact the person's doctor for advice.

Appropriate help *can* reduce the risk of a very unhappy person completing suicide. So if the person openly talks about suicide, then don't just dismiss what they are saying and refuse to take it seriously. Do not try to make a joke of it, or tell them not to be 'silly'. Above all, at this time, they want to be taken seriously, and feel understood and listened to. Accepting what they are saying and trying to empathize is so important. If you discover that the person has actually thought about *how* they would kill themselves, then you must take it very seriously indeed. The more detailed the plan, the more likely the person may be to make an attempt. In this situation you may need to get urgent help or advice from a doctor.

But this advice does not ignore the emotional dilemmas you may find yourself facing. You may start from the moral standpoint that someone has the right to end his or her own life and may wonder if you have the right to intervene. The priority is to get proper help for the depression rather than be drawn into the justification for suicide, which may stem from symptoms of depression that have not been treated.

Another dilemma may be that if you summon any kind of outside help you may jeopardize your relationship with that person. Realistically, this is a risk you must be aware of. However, it is important to remember that most people who attempt suicide are suffering from treatable mental distress.

Ultimately, of course, the decision to take one's own life rests with that individual. Even if you summon help, it is very important to realize that you still cannot prevent anyone from taking their own life if they are determined to do so. And if someone does take their own life, it is *their* ultimate responsibility. It is not your fault. If you try to persuade them to get help or seek help on their behalf and they refuse to accept help, then there is nothing you can do about it. Bear in mind that under the Mental Health Act 1983 a person can be treated without their consent; so this may be a last resort, but must be considered very carefully. It is not an easy option for anyone involved.

Even if a suicide attempt is averted, it is important to remember that it won't automatically make the problems the person had that led up to the suicide attempt disappear. On-going help and support is vital; if the underlying problems can be addressed, then it is less likely that suicidal feelings will return.

9

How to look after *you*

When you are concerned about someone you love, whether they have depression or any other illness or health problem, the temptation all too often is to put them first and yourself last. You reason that you feel well, so it seems wrong to spend even one moment worrying about, or caring for, yourself. If you are a woman you may feel this even more strongly, because of the way women are so often associated with the 'caring' role.

There are two main reasons why it's a good idea for you to look after yourself. First, if you take time out to recharge your batteries, then you will be better able to help the person you love who has depression. And the second reason? Because you count too. You shouldn't ignore your own mental, emotional and physical health just because you feel OK at the moment. If you don't look after your own health now, then you are setting yourself up for the possibility of becoming ill later – and that won't help either of you.

Depression can be all-consuming for a family, but you are entitled to a life too. You may feel that your circumstances are such that you simply can't take time off or devote energy to yourself; maybe you feel too tired even to think about doing so because all your energy goes into worrying about the person who has depression, or caring for them. You may even feel that you are strong, tough and can cope – that there's no need to make a point of looking after yourself. Maybe, deep down, you are worried that if you stop, then you won't be able to start again; if you think about yourself even for a moment, you might start crying and never stop; that if you let up, then you might want to lie down and would find it too difficult to get up again; that if you pause for breath, then you'll be too tired to continue the journey.

All these fears and worries are understandable; but if you are thinking like this, then there is even more reason to rethink your routine and take just a little time out for yourself.

If you are a carer, you may think it's unrealistic. If *you* aren't there, then who else would be there to do what needs to be done? And who could do it as well? In order to take a break, you have to get through this claustrophobic line of argument and aim to be less than perfect just once in a while – aim to be merely 'good enough' instead.

And lest you think we're talking here of six weeks in the Bahamas or a world cruise, let's not get carried away! The reality for many carers is that a 'break' might just be the chance to put your feet up for half-an-hour reading the paper – uninterrupted. Or perhaps the opportunity of a really long soak in the bath without feeling guilty, a morning at the shops when you aren't already planning the chores for the rest of the day or, luxury of luxuries, just a day doing nothing much in particular except pottering about, with no phones going, no demands on your time, no reason to talk to anyone, let alone give advice or sympathy; in other words, a few moments free of worrying, wondering, feeling anxious or guilty, concerned you haven't done enough or have done too much, free from the tyranny of thinking you 'should' do this or that.

One survey conducted by St John Ambulance has found that levels of stress, depression and illness in carers are rising. Nearly one-third of carers say they are suffering from stress or depression or both; and nearly half say they are suffering from chronic fatigue. It is often the emotional exhaustion that is so draining: the sheer relentlessness of the job; having to worry day in, day out; wanting to do your best and fearing it is never quite good enough.

There are so many mixed feelings to make sense of – one minute you can feel incredible sympathy for the depressed person's plight – but then feel irritated because they don't want to talk or seem down for no good reason. You know they aren't 'putting it on' or behaving like that just to annoy you, yet there are times you may well feel like crying 'what about me?' You may get tired of living in the midst of depression all the time and long to have a conversation about something ordinary for a change. And if you know you are the main lifeline for the person who is depressed, then the strain can be relentless and huge. It won't help if the person you spend so much time caring for isn't very grateful either! And the fact you are trying to help someone doesn't necessarily mean they want your help or agree that you are helping in the right way. Their illness may even mean they are suspicious of your motives, and aggressive or resentful of things you say or do.

You may feel guilty that you are not doing enough; that you

should take on more responsibility; or perhaps you would like to withdraw and back off, but don't know how? You may also feel angry or resentful that it is you who seems to shoulder most of the burden while others in the family are not doing their bit.

Finding a way through all this will inevitably be difficult. But however much you love or care for someone else, you too have a right to a life – and if *you* become ill through giving, giving, giving, then it won't help either of you.

Ultimately, you can only do what you can do – you can do your best, no more and no less. Don't waste energy trying to get others to take responsibility – you can't make anyone else do anything they don't want to. You can only take responsibility for yourself. Be honest with yourself and others about what you can and can't offer, what you can and can't do. Try not to get angry if others in the family are not doing what you consider to be their 'fair share'. Having an argument about it probably won't change anything – it will just make you feel more upset. You may long for a break and feel others in the family should automatically know how you feel and offer to do more. But perhaps they don't know. Or perhaps they do know, but just can't face getting involved. Whatever the rights and wrongs, analysing and fretting about their reasons won't make you feel any better or help the situation. Allow others to make – and live with – their own decisions.

If you are a carer, finding time for yourself can seem a low priority, not least because in addition to your role as a carer, you are probably juggling other aspects of your own life. But even the smallest changes can help you feel a whole lot better and give you renewed energy to fight another day.

So how can you look after yourself? These ideas may help:

- Try to keep up your own circle of friends. With so many commitments it's easy to let things slide, but friends can be an enormous source of support. This is especially important if you are a man – women tend to have more friends and acquaintances, but if you're not the kind of man who is happy to wander into a pub and you don't belong to any social or sports clubs, it can be difficult.
- When you are with friends, try to talk about things other than depression. It is good to 'get things off your chest', but you also

need to have a good time, a bit of a laugh, and just a break away from it all from time to time.

- Don't try to hide from friends what you are going through. You may not want to splurge all your emotions or be seen to want sympathy, but on the other hand there may be times when you have to refuse invitations because of your role as a carer, however informal, and it may be as well to explain to friends that if you refuse invitations, it is not necessarily because you don't want to go.
- Learn how to say 'no' so that you don't waste time doing things you dislike or meeting people you don't care for – save your energy for the people you do care for.
- Do treat yourself from time to time – and only you know what constitutes a treat. If you do organize something for yourself, then enjoy it – and refuse to feel guilty about either the time or the money you spend on yourself once in a while. You deserve it.
- Learn to relax with simple relaxation exercises. For example, tense and relax each set of muscles in turn, starting at the forehead, mouth, throat, neck, shoulders and so on down to the calves, ankles, feet and toes. Make a point of taking one minute every half-hour or hour (if you work at a computer you may be able to program it to bleep on cue) to stand up, take three deep breaths, and breathe out a long, slow, breath. Be aware of how you are – if you are rushing around, then make a conscious effort to slow down, take stock. Do you really need to get tensed up and be so frantic? Find something to savour and enjoy and divert your attention for a few minutes – the pattern of the clouds, the swaying of trees in a breeze, the smell of a garden flower.
- If the person in your life who has depression is not your partner, you may have to justify the time and care you are giving that person to others in the family, especially to your own partner. You may feel guilty about the time you are spending with them, and it may be causing arguments or an atmosphere at home. This situation is so difficult, and you probably feel torn in two: wanting to do the best for everyone, yet feeling drained and exhausted because of all the effort you are putting in. Navigating your way around this situation is not easy – and it may be impossible to please everyone. In order to get a balance in your

life, you may have to accept that you can't be perfect. Decide what your priorities are – not just short-term, but long-term too. Do not allow sentiment and sympathy to cloud your judgement – strike a balance between the needs of the person who is depressed, the other people in your life who have needs too, and your own needs. *Remember: you count too*! Aim for 'good enough' rather than absolutely perfect.

Such changes may sound trite and not appropriate for you. This doesn't matter. *You* know yourself best, and can make up your own mind as to how you can take time out to recharge your batteries to the greatest effect.

10

Understanding treatments for depression

Antidepressants

If someone you love has depression and is prescribed antidepressants, you may want to know a little about them.

First, according to the World Health Organization, antidepressant drugs are effective for both moderate and severe depression (World Health Report, 2001). It says they can be effective even in the case of mild depression. Overall, the World Health Organization estimates a success rate of about 70 per cent. However, according to MIND (in *Making Sense of Antidepressants*), research shows that in 40 per cent of people a placebo is equally effective – which means it is difficult to generalize about who would benefit most from taking antidepressants. MIND says that a high proportion of people with depression recover spontaneously without treatment.

Nevertheless, doctors tend to take the view that antidepressants should be the first choice of treatment in most patients with major depression, as well as in persistent minor depression or dysthymia – although psychological treatments such as cognitive therapy or counselling may be offered as well. Anyone who has 'psychotic' symptoms, such as hearing voices, is likely to be referred to a psychiatrist as a matter of urgency.

The eminent clinical psychologist Dorothy Rowe, renowned around the world for her work on depression and the author of several highly successful books (see Further Reading), advises that anyone who is taking drugs for depression would do well to know enough about them to 'feel in control of them', e.g. what type of pills they are, the effects they are supposed to have, the side-effects, and how they might affect your life. She points out that antidepressants and tranquillizers do not remove the cause of the pain, but simply reduce the amount of pain. 'There are no wonder drugs,' she cautions.

There are three main types of antidepressants:

• Tricyclic antidepressants (TCAs) and related antidepressants.

- Selective serotonin reuptake inhibitors (SSRIs) and related antidepressants.
- Monoamine oxidase inhibitors (MAOIs).

In addition there is lithium, which is often used in cases of manic depression, and some new drug treatments as well. But what are these drugs and how do they work? First, we have to take a closer look at the chemistry of the brain.

How do antidepressants work?

The brain is extremely complex and comprises millions of neurons, or brain cells. Every action in the body, our thoughts, perceptions, actions and feelings, are the result of the activity of millions of neurons in the brain. Information is brought to the brain via the neurons and carried by neurons to the rest of the body along axons. If you reach for a cup of coffee, the thought and the action starts with activity by the neurons in the brain. Neurons convey all this information via short pulses of electricity along the axons. Information is carried between the neurons, or between a neuron and a muscle, by means of chemical messengers called neurotransmitters. The gap between neurons is called a 'synapse' and it's the neurotransmitter's job to bridge the synapse or gap between the neurons. A neurotransmitter is stored at the terminal of a neuron and only released as a result of the electrical impulse.

After it has 'jumped' the synapse or gap, the neurotransmitter then binds to specialized receptors on the other side of the synapse or gap, causing the second neuron to continue the pulse of electricity. If the neurotransmitter isn't released for some reason, then the target (for example, the brain or an individual muscle) wouldn't receive the intended information.

After the neurotransmitter has jumped the gap, it is either taken back into the terminal of the first neuron (called 'reuptake'), and conserved for future use, or it is processed into waste by the synapse. If this does not happen, then too much neurotransmitter stays in the synapse, potentially sending too strong a signal to the second neuron.

So how does all this relate to depression and to antidepressants? Scientists have discovered that depression is sometimes associated

94

with low levels of particular neurotransmitters such as norepineph-rine (noradrenaline) and serotonin (sometimes called 5-hydroxy-tryptamine or 5-HT).

Tricyclic drugs (TCAs) (they're called tricyclic because of their chemical structure, which comprises three chains) work by preventing the reuptake of norepinephrine or serotonin by the 'first' neuron's terminal. The rationale is that if the depression is linked to low levels of one of the neurotransmitters in the brain, then preventing 'reuptake' means more of the neurotransmitter will remain in the synapse to ensure it stimulates the second, and so on.

Monoamine oxidase inhibitors (MAOIs) work by preventing the synapse from recycling or degrading the neurotransmitter – monoamine oxidase is just the name of the enzyme involved in the degrading process. Again, this means that more of the neurotrans-mitter remains in the synapse to ensure it stimulates the second, and so on.

TCAs and MAOIs work on two neurotransmitters – norepin-ephrine and serotonin. For a long time, scientists were not sure which of the two was the most important in terms of depression. But a newer class of drugs, called selective serotonin reuptake inhibitors (SSRIs), have now been developed (Prozac is the most well known) that target only serotonin, as some scientists believe this is the more important neurotransmitter.

How does a doctor decide which antidepressants to prescribe for a patient? In general, TCAs and SSRIs are chosen, especially for patients who have never taken antidepressants before. A doctor would take into account various factors such as any medication a patient was already on for pre-existing medical conditions; the side-effects of the drugs being considered; how sleepy the drugs would make a patient feel, and how that might help or hinder the course of the depression; how likely the patient was to attempt suicide; and how likely the patient was to remember to take the drugs. If someone has had an episode of depression in the past and it recurs, then the drug used last time might be prescribed again, especially if there were no problems previously.

It is important to be aware that although most antidepressants have a similar potential to be effective, an antidepressant that works for one person may not be as effective for someone else. Similarly, although a particular drug may be known for having certain side-effects, not everyone will experience the same side-effects to the same intensity. So every patient is treated individually. It may be that a particular drug's side-effects could actually work to a person's benefit – for example, if the person suffers from insomnia, then an antidepressant that tends to be sedating is likely to be a more sensible choice than a non-sedative drug.

Tricyclic antidepressants (TCAs)

TCAs tend to be given for moderate to severe (endogenous) depression when a doctor cannot pinpoint a specific cause for depression, and where symptoms such as loss of appetite and sleep disturbance are present. Some TCAs are also given when someone is experiencing panic attacks.

Important note
Some TCAs:

- can cause drowsiness, so may affect a person's ability to drive or operate machinery; but some antidepressants are more likely to cause drowsiness than others, so it is worth discussing this with the doctor if it is a concern;
- are not suitable for people who have heart problems, or severe liver disease;
- may not be suitable for people who have diabetes, heart, liver or thyroid disease, epilepsy, glaucoma or kidney problems;
- may not be taken with certain tranquillizers;
- may not be taken with the herbal remedy St John's Wort as it will cause an adverse reaction.

There may be other contraindications too, so it is important to discuss medication with the doctor and to ensure that all the facts are known. In general, low doses of TCAs would be prescribed initially, and then increased every three to seven days, according to how well they are tolerated, until the minimum effective dose is reached. The elderly are more susceptible to side-effects (particularly sleepiness and low blood pressure), so the doses should be increased more slowly.

Often, these drugs can be taken just once a day – usually at night, but this may vary. A doctor should normally see someone who has been prescribed TCAs every week or two weeks for the first month or so in order to see how they are getting on, whether there are any side-effects, and to assess whether the person feels better or worse.

In general, TCAs and related antidepressants can be broadly split into those that tend to have a sedative effect and those that are less so. If someone is anxious, they are more likely to be prescribed a sedative type – this may sound worrying, as though the patient is somehow being sedated deliberately. But anxious and agitated patients do tend to respond best to the more sedative type of TCA.

Examples of TCAs and related antidepressants that tend to be more sedative include:

- amitriptyline hydrochloride
- clomipramine
- dosulepin
- doxepin
- maprotiline
- mianserin
- trazodone
- trimipramine.

Those that have less sedative potential include:

- amoxapine
- imipramine
- lofepramine
- nortriptyline.

Don't forget these are the *generic* names – in some cases, there may be several different brand names.

What other side-effects can you expect, apart from sleepiness or drowsiness? Dry mouth, constipation, blurred vision, sweating and urinary retention are some. The elderly may suffer dizziness. Less common, but more serious, side effects include arrhythmias (when the heart beats irregularly) and heart block, which in rare cases, where someone has pre-existing heart disease, can cause sudden death. Convulsions are another rare side-effect, which is why these drugs are avoided for those with epilepsy. If the person you love is worried about side-effects, then encourage them to discuss this with their doctor.

Selective serotonin reuptake inhibitors (SSRIs)

This group of antidepressants works on the neurotransmitter called serotonin. It works by blocking the reuptake of serotonin (5-hydroxytryptamine, 5-HT) into the nerve cell that released it. This effectively prolongs the action of the neurotransmitter. This group of drugs tend not to produce the same side-effects as the TCAs, such as dry mouth and constipation, and are less likely to cause heart problems if taken in overdose; but they may cause nausea, vomiting and other side-effects, though they are less sedating than the TCAs. Doctors may prefer not to prescribe an SSRI – for example, if someone has epilepsy or the person is in a manic phase. Also, the SSRIs are not necessarily more effective than the TCAs. (Some doctors prefer to initially prescribe a TCA rather than an SSRI.)

As with other antidepressants, abrupt withdrawal from SSRIs can produce unpleasant side-effects, so it must be done slowly and under medical supervision.

Examples of SSRIs include:

• citalopram
• escitalopram
• fluoxetine
• fluvoxamine
• paroxetine
• sertraline.

There are also several antidepressants that are SSRI-related and work slightly differently to those mentioned above – for example, nefazodone hydrochloride.

SSRIs are a newer group of antidepressants than the TCAs and MAOIs, and one in particular – fluoxetine (brand name Prozac) – is widely used and has received an enormous amount of coverage in the press. However, some SSRIs – for example, paroxetine (brand name Seroxat) – have been linked by some research to a possible increase in suicide, so if the person you love is prescribed any of the drugs in the SSRI group it is essential to discuss this aspect with their doctor and find out what the latest advice is.

Monoamine oxidase inhibitors (MAOIs)

This group of drugs works on the same neurotransmitters as the TCAs – noradrenaline and serotonin – but in a different way. MAOIs are used far less frequently than the TCAs or SSRIs (and their related antidepressants) because of the increased likelihood of adverse interactions with other drugs, and also with some foods. This group of drugs tends to have more side-effects than the TCAs, and so they are usually prescribed if other types of antidepressants have failed. In cases of severe depression, MAOIs may be less effective than the TCAs. According to the British National Formulary, some psychiatrists use selected TCAs in conjunction with MAOIs, but it also says that this is 'harzardous', and even potentially lethal, and there is no evidence that the combination is more effective. The British National Formulary also says the combination of tranylcypromine with clomipramine is particularly dangerous.

Examples of MAOIs include:

- phenelzine
- isocarboxazid
- tranylcypromine – generally considered to be the least safe in this group.

Because some of the drugs in this group affect the way certain foods are digested, if the person you love is prescribed one of the MAOIs, they have to be very careful to avoid these foods as they can become poisonous to the body. Full information should be given with the drugs. What happens is that food that has been exposed to air and is no longer fresh, either because it is a fruit left to over-ripen or food that has been pickled, cured or dried, for instance, causes raised levels of a chemical called tyramine, which interacts with MAOI drugs to make those foods poisonous to the body – causing a dangerous rise in blood pressure. Examples of foods that must be avoided are Marmite, Bovril, Oxo, alcohol, non-alcoholic beers and lagers, mature cheese, pickled herrings, broad bean pods, fermented soya bean extract and over-ripe fruit. Any food suspected of being old or stale, such as less than fresh meat or fish, should be avoided. Game should also be avoided. Fresh foods are best. It is important to get accurate information about this as if someone on MAOIs does eat the wrong kind of food, it can be fatal. Although this is rare, it can happen – so do find out as much as you can. One early warning sign of this food interaction with MAOI drugs is a throbbing headache.

How long do antidepressants take to work?

How long do antidepressants take to work? Some improvement should be seen after four weeks – and it is very important to stress that the patient (or their loved ones) is unlikely to see any response at all for at least two weeks. The full effect may not be apparent until six weeks. Improvement obviously depends on the patient having taken the drug regularly at the dose specified.

Most people are prescribed antidepressants for between four and six months, although a significant study which looked at data from 31 different trials, including a total of over 4,000 patients, suggested that longer-term use of antidepressants – a year or more rather than the standard 4–6-month treatment – could substantially reduce the risk of a relapse for people with depression.

If there is no or little improvement, as can happen in about 10–20 per cent of patients, the doctor may suggest changing the antidepressants. If this is done, then the usual practice is to gradually reduce one drug and slowly introduce a different one – but this is not always the case, and the patient must be guided by the doctor. For example, if someone has been taking a TCA and the doctor wants to try a MAOI instead, it is likely there would be a gap of up to 14 days between the stopping of the TCA and the starting of the MAOI. Again, the doctor should work closely with the patient to ensure the dose is high enough to make a difference, but not so high as to cause severe side-effects (BNF, 2002).

About a third of patients relapse within a year of remission from depression, and research shows that antidepressants should be continued for at least four to six months after recovery as there is strong evidence that this will help prevent a relapse (Geddes et al., 2000). Elderly patients may benefit from continued treatment for at least 12 months.

If the person you love has recurrent depression, then they may be put on a 'maintenance dose', as this may help to reduce the risk of recurrence. Indeed, some people may need to stay on medication indefinitely.

Once a person has started on antidepressants and has been on them regularly for at least six weeks, it is very important that they do not stop taking them abruptly as this may cause serious withdrawal side-effects. In some cases, the dose can be gradually reduced over a period of two to four weeks – or longer in other cases.

Some other drugs used in the treatment of depression

- Noradrenergic and specific serotonergic antidepressants (NaSSAs). There is one main drug in this group that is similar to the tricyclic group of drugs. It works on two neurotransmitters, noradrenaline and serotonin. It is a newer drug that may have fewer side-effects than the older tricyclics. An example of a NaSSA is mirtazapine – brand name Zispin.
- The drug flupentixol (brand name Fluanxol) is also sometimes given as an antidepressant or used in the treatment of psychosis. Other drugs that may be given include tryptophan and venlafaxine.
- Anxiolytics (sometimes called tranquillizers) such as the benzodiazepines (diazepam) are used to induce sleep, and they can be of great value to someone in the short term if they are finding it impossible to sleep during a stressful period (e.g. after a bereavement). They are prescribed widely, but physical and psychological dependence is a worrying consequence of overuse. In addition, patients become 'tolerant' to the drug, so greater doses are needed to achieve the same effect. Withdrawal symptoms can arise if someone stops taking these drugs after having taken them regularly for just a few weeks. One problem is that if someone does try to withdraw from taking a drug like diazepam, they may experience withdrawal symptoms that mirror the symptoms they originally started to take the drug for – anxiety and insomnia, for example – and that can lead them into thinking that they need to carry on taking the drug. Time

UNDERSTANDING TREATMENTS FOR DEPRESSION

needed for withdrawal can vary from four weeks to over a year, and it has to be done very slowly indeed. Other benzodiazepines include loprazolam, chlordiazepoxide, lorazepam, nitrazepam and temazepam. Prevailing advice is that benzodiazepines should be used for no more than two to four weeks.

- Lithium. This drug is often used in the treatment of manic depression, and sometimes in recurrent depression too. It is also used in extreme cases where someone is highly aggressive or self-harming. Lithium can cause gastro-intestinal and other more serious side-effects, including brain damage, if the dosage is too high. It is sometimes given with an anti-psychotic drug – although as the lithium becomes effective, the anti-psychotic may be slowly withdrawn. A woman thinking of becoming pregnant, or suddenly finding she is pregnant, should discuss with her doctor whether it is safe to be on lithium. It is important also to discuss diet with a doctor, as it is essential when taking this drug to ensure the right balance of fluid and salt intake.
- Carbamazepine (Tegretol). This is sometimes used to treat manic depression, or as a preventative measure in this illness, if lithium has not been effective.

One meta-analysis (a study that analyses the results of lots of studies) (Gill and Hatcher, 1999) looked at 18 randomized controlled trials of antidepressants versus placebos, or no therapy at all, in people who had both depression and a physical illness. It shows that patients on antidepressants were significantly more likely to improve than those in the other groups studied.

Anti-psychotic drugs

These drugs are sometimes called 'major tranquillizers', but according to MIND, this term is very misleading as these drugs do not make people feel calm and often produce severe restlessness. It is thought they work by blocking dopamine receptors in the brain.

Anti-psychotics (sometimes called 'neuroleptics') are mostly prescribed for schizophrenia and psychotic states – psychosis is a state where a person experiences hallucinations and delusions. In

some cases, they relieve acute anxiety and control severe aggressive and manic behaviour.
Examples of anti-psychotic drugs include:

- chlorpromazine
- pericyazine
- fluphenazine
- thioxanthenes
- loxapine.

Newer anti-psychotic drugs include:

- amisulpride
- clozapine
- olanzapine
- risperiodone
- sertindole
- zotepine.

It is unlikely that someone suffering from mild or moderate depression (or even severe depression) would be prescribed an antipsychotic drug. If they are, then they and you may wish to discuss this further with your doctor.

Important notes about antidepressants

- Remember that all drugs have 'non-proprietary' or 'generic' names, which are recognized internationally, and also 'brand' names. Several pharmaceutical companies may sell a particular non-proprietary drug, such as one of those listed above, but may have created their own brand name. For example, fluoxetine has the brand name of Prozac, and paroxetine has the brand name of Seroxat.
- Not all antidepressants mentioned are suitable for children.
- Some antidepressants are contra-indicated for the elderly or for those suffering from certain illnesses or health problems, such as diabetes, heart, liver or thyroid disease, or if you are pregnant or thinking about becoming pregnant. It is very important that

103

drugs are prescribed only by a doctor who knows the person's full medical history.

- It is very dangerous to exceed the dose prescribed.
- It is dangerous to *suddenly* stop taking the prescribed dose – this should be done only gradually and in consultation with a doctor.
- If you are worried that the person you love has stopped taking their antidepressants, signs of withdrawal can include nausea, abdominal pain, vomiting, diarrhoea, chills, weakness, sweating, fatigue, headache and anxiety, as well as feeling generally unwell. 'Manic' behaviour and an inability to sleep may also occur in some people.
- Older antidepressants (TCAs known as ADTs) have been shown to be just as effective as newer drugs on the market, although newer antidepressant drugs may have fewer side-effects.

Questions to ask a doctor about prescribed drugs

1 What is the name of the drug being prescribed?
2 What kind of drug is it?
3 How will the drug help?
4 How often should it be taken?
5 At what times should it be taken and are there any special instructions as to how (e.g. before, with, or after meals)?
6 How long should the drug be taken for?
7 How important is it to take the drug?
8 What happens if the person forgets to take the drug?
9 What are the most common side-effects?
10 What other side-effects might occur?
11 Is it OK to drive while taking this drug?
12 Is this drug suitable for taking with other medications that have been prescribed?
13 Is it OK to drink alcohol while taking this drug?
14 If pregnant or thinking about becoming pregnant, is it still OK to take this drug?
15 How long will it take for this drug to be effective?

Some people worry about being referred to a psychiatrist. In most cases of depression this is not necessary, but if the depression is severe, your GP may prefer to refer you.

What about ECT?

Electro Convulsive Therapy (ECT) has always been a controversial treatment. It is used for severe depression if other treatments have not worked, as well as for other types of mental illness, such as schizophrenia.

So what is the rationale behind the use of ECT? When a brain is functioning properly, the millions of cells in the brain work together, fired by 'neurotransmitters' – chemicals that relay information from one cell to another. The electrical impulses that travel along each nerve cell are carried over a microscopic gap, called a synapse, by these chemical messengers, the neurotransmitters. If the chemistry of the brain becomes unbalanced it is because the neurotransmitters or chemicals are not firing between one cell and another – and lowering of mood or depression may be one of the results.

As we noted earlier, we know that certain chemical neurotransmitters, such as serotonin, are lowered in depression – though it is not known why. ECT is a way of 're-firing' the neurotransmitters and restoring a connection between cells. In some depressed people, this can have a dramatic effect on mood and lift them out of depression sufficiently for them to resume a normal life.

There are two ways of administering ECT. Bilateral ECT involves placing one electrode on each temple, whereas unilateral ECT involves placing two electrodes on one temple. It is important to discuss the differences with your doctor, and you can find out more from *The ECT Handbook*, published by the Royal College of Psychiatrists.

There is no doubt that the idea of ECT is scary – most people have seen the frightening images as portrayed in films like *One Flew Over the Cuckoo's Nest*. On the other hand, it may offer a useful form of treatment, particularly for someone who feels suicidal, when other types of treatment have failed, or if someone is so depressed they are refusing to eat or drink. But, according to MIND, although it has been a life-saver for some people, others feel the long-term side-effects to be an 'unacceptable consequence'.

What happens is that the patient is given a short-acting general anaesthetic and a muscle relaxant to stop convulsions during treatment. Electrodes are attached via pads that are placed either side (or the same side) of the skull and an electric current is then delivered to the brain. Effectively, the electric shock causes the patient's muscles to contract or convulse vigorously, inducing a kind of fit that is akin to an epileptic fit. This has the effect of triggering the neurotransmitters to work again.

ECT may be given once or twice a week for six or eight weeks. Although ECT is thought to act on the neurotransmitters in the brain, it is not really understood *exactly* how it works. One controversial theory is that ECT works by causing brain damage. Nevertheless, ECT may offer a rapid improvement of symptoms.

There are many possible side-effects of ECT. In the MIND survey, which was based on 418 respondents, some short-term side-effects (lasting up to six weeks) were, in order of frequency: headaches, drowsiness, confusion, loss of past memories, dizziness, disorientation, difficulty in concentrating, and inability to remember new information. Permanent side-effects were, in order of frequency: loss of past memories, difficulty in concentrating, fear or anxiety, an inability to remember new information, feelings of worthlessness, and feelings of helplessness.

In addition, ECT may cause damage to the teeth or mouth. According to MIND, ECT can have an emotional impact too, and this is under-researched and not often discussed. In MIND's survey, an astonishing 22 per cent of people who had recently received ECT felt they were being 'punished'.

According to *The ECT Handbook* by the Royal College of Psychiatrists (see Further Reading), someone may refuse to have ECT and may withdraw their consent at any time, even before the first treatment has been given. Signing a 'consent form' does not mean you have to have the treatment – it is a record that an explanation has been given about the treatment and that you understand what is going to happen, but it doesn't mean you have to have the treatment just because you have signed the form. However, ECT can be given without consent if you have been 'sectioned' or detained in hospital under the Mental Health Act 1983, when it can be authorized by a doctor appointed by the Mental Health Act Commission.

MIND found in a survey conducted in 2001 that 36 per cent of those who had received ECT in the previous five years had found it helpful within the first six weeks of treatment; 27 per cent found it unhelpful or damaging in the short term; and 43 per cent felt it was unhelpful or damaging in the long term. MIND reported that two thirds of all those asked, and almost half of those who had had ECT in the previous two years, would not agree to have it again.

On the other hand, the Royal College of Psychiatrists point to a study of ECT in Scotland which indicates that over the last six years, over 70 per cent of patients who have had ECT improve significantly and go on to lead normal lives (Royal College of Psychiatrists press release). Another piece of research reviewed a variety of studies to see how safe and effective ECT is for patients with depression. It concluded that ECT is an effective short-term treatment for depression, and probably more effective than drug therapy. It found that bilateral ECT is moderately more effective than unilateral ECT and high-dose ECT is more effective than a low dose (Geddes, 2003). Nonetheless, ECT remains a controversial treatment.

New treatments for the future

According to the Mayo Clinic in the USA, many new treatments for depression are being investigated. These include:

- *Transcranial magnetic stimulation* (TMS). In this, an electrical current is passed from a hand-held device, which is simply held against the head, via a wire coil. The current creates a magnetic pulse which stimulates nerve cells in the brain. The patient does not need to be anaesthetized during the procedure, and a big advantage is that it is not thought to generally cause memory loss. One day, TMS may become a common treatment for depression and may even replace ECT, although at the moment trials are still in a very early stage.
- *Vagal nerve stimulation* (VNS). The vagus nerve connects the brain to other organs in the body. The vagal nerve can be stimulated by inserting a small device in the chest – rather like a pacemaker for the heart. Small wires go from the device up to the neck where it is connected to the vagus nerve and electrical pulses are programmed to stimulate the nerve. It is thought that this may improve symptoms of depression. The technique was originally developed to treat people with epilepsy, and it was

noted that in addition to reducing seizures, the treatment seemed to improve mood – although it's not known why. But in the future it may offer a treatment for some people with depression. For more information from the Mayo Clinic, see the website at *www.mayoclinic.com*

Dealing with doctors

When someone you love has depression, of course it is he or she who is ill, not you. This can present problems if you want to find out about what treatments they have been prescribed, how severe their doctor thinks the depression is, and what their prognosis is. You may be filled with dozens of questions – How long are they likely to be ill? Will they need to go into hospital? What caused the depression? Will the treatments work? What are the side-effects likely to be? If the depression recurs, will it eventually get better? What should you do if the person forgets to take their medication? Will counselling help? – and so on.

To a large extent, you will have to rely on what the person who is depressed tells you – and the very nature of depression means that they may not be able to tell you very much at all, or recall all the details you want to know; this can be very frustrating, or even annoying, though it is understandable.

If you are the person's partner, or parent or grown-up offspring, and the person concerned is happy to let you accompany them to the doctor, then you may find the doctor is more than happy to put you in the picture and answer all your questions. But, if not, then the issue of doctor/patient confidentiality is liable to come between you and the information you need.

It is highly unlikely that if you phone the doctor you will be given any information, and this may be irritating. After all, you may reason that if you are the one who has to live with the person, then you are entitled to know what's wrong with them and how long they are likely to be ill, and so on.

If the doctor refuses to speak to you, then you will have to be guided by what the person who is depressed tells you and be satisfied with that. On the other hand, you may find the person welcomes the opportunity of you attending the doctors' appointments with them.

If you *are* asked to accompany someone who is depressed when they visit a doctor, what is the best way to approach the situation?

- First, do check out the rules and regulations of the doctor's practice – opening times etc. – and respect them.
- Avoid asking for a home visit unless it is absolutely necessary.
- Don't be afraid to take in a list of questions and write down key points of the answers.
- If you think you might want to offer comments about what the person who is depressed is going to say, or give additional information, ask them first if this is OK.
- If you do not understand what the doctor is saying, then say so – and don't be afraid to ask them to repeat an explanation.
- You may want to ask about medications – how long they take to work, side-effects, etc. For more information about this, see page 93.

Efficacy of counselling and other therapies versus drug treatment

Counselling, cognitive behavioural therapy and time-limited inter-personal psychotherapy have all been shown to be potentially as effective as drugs in mild to moderate depression. Knowing this is very important if you live with someone who has depression, as you will probably already know yourself that someone who is depressed may not seek help for themselves simply because some of the symptoms of depression, such as lack of energy and lack of motivation, make seeking help very difficult – which is a great shame given that counselling and other talking therapies are known to be of enormous help. Of course, you can't make someone go for counselling – and it is unlikely that you will be able to make an appointment on their behalf. All you can do is encourage and help to motivate the person who is depressed – and then leave the decision to him or her. (There is more about this subject in Chapter 12.)

Treatments for older people

Research shows that older people are more sensitive to the side-effects of drugs than younger people are, so an initial dose of any drug is liable to be prescribed at a low dosage to see how well it works, and then increased very gradually (Wilson and Curran, 2001).

Many doctors will avoid the traditional monoamine oxidase inhibitor drugs (MAOIs) and the older trycyclic drugs (TCAs) such as amitriptyline, as they can cause side-effects. Newer TCAs such as lofepramine, or the selective serotonin reuptake inhibitor drugs (SSRIs), are more likely to be better tolerated.

It has been suggested (Wilson and Curran, 2001) that the elderly have a high risk of a recurrence following a depressive episode, and they point to research that shows a 70 per cent risk of recurrence within two years of remission. This, together with other factors, means that a doctor may recommend that an older person needs to continue treatment for at least one year, and maybe even up to two years, after recovery.

ECT is thought to be a safe, effective treatment for older patients who are too ill for alternative treatments, or fail to respond to them; and the response rate is between 70 and 80 per cent (Flint, 1992). One factor worth considering if you are worried about ECT is that if ECT is considered a last resort and the person then responds well to ECT, they may then be in a position to take advantage of other therapies that may help them to stay well (Benbow, 2001).

11

The importance of diet and exercise

We all know that good nutrition is important for health and well-being, but the importance of diet as a factor in illness is still in its infancy. The World Health Organization has only recently suggested that diet may be a key factor in up to a third of all cancers, and we already know that diet plays a role in a variety of medical conditions from diabetes to heart disease.

The notion that food can affect our emotional well-being and mental health is controversial. But though it is not easy to conduct convincing scientific studies to show that diet is directly linked to depression, some studies offer interesting results, for example:

* Reducing sugar and caffeine may help lift mood.
* Eating a diet rich in omega 3 fatty acids (for example, oily fish like salmon or mackerel) may help to reduce depression.
* Ensuring an adequate intake of vitamin B12 may help too – a deficiency in this vitamin can cause anaemia, which is linked to depression, but a lack of vitamin B12 may exacerbate depression even if anaemia is not present.
* Studies have suggested that taking a vitamin B6 supplement may help some women who have symptoms of depression.
* Low levels of selenium have also been linked to depression.

(You can read more about diet at *www.gnc.com*)

Links between depression and diet

There is anecdotal evidence as to how food and mood may be linked. MIND, for instance, conducted a survey in 2002 that showed that everyday changes to diet can have a positive and sometimes rapid effect on mental health. This organization surveyed 200 people on their database and found that 88 per cent were using self-help strategies to monitor and control their diet in order to improve their emotional well-being. Of those using this form of self-help, 80 per cent found that cutting down or avoiding sugar had a beneficial effect on mental health; 79 per cent cited caffeine as being detrimental; 55 per cent cited alcohol; and 53 per cent said chocolate. As well as cutting back on these 'food stressors', some had found certain foods to be beneficial – drinking more water was mentioned by 80 per cent, 78 per cent mentioned vegetables, 72 per cent said fruit, and 52 per cent said oily fish.

The MIND survey also asked what changes in eating patterns had been the most effective. The researchers discovered that eating regular meals and snacks, not missing breakfast, and people being prepared by carrying healthy snacks with them when out (to avoid sudden drops in blood sugar levels) were the best strategies for feeling better.

Diet may be an area you could talk about with the person you love who has depression. Although everyone is an individual, some common foods that may contribute to greater anxiety, irritability, difficulty in concentrating, tiredness, hyperactivity, difficulties in sleeping and aggression – in themselves all possible symptoms of depression, as well as lowering of mood – include:

- chocolate
- coffee
- oranges
- artificial additives, e.g. E numbers, flavourings and preservatives
- sugar
- wheat
- dairy products
- eggs.

One study suggests that a diet deficient in folate is linked to depression, persistent depressive symptoms and a poor response to antidepressants (Bjelland et al., 2003). So eating more folate-rich foods such as fortified breakfast cereals, brussels sprouts, peanuts, okra, almonds and liver, or taking a supplement, could be of value.

What kind of diet is best?

Ten tips

1 Aim for five portions of fruit and vegetables a day. However, potatoes don't count towards your five portions, and fruit juice only counts once, no matter how many glasses you drink. So

what counts as a 'portion'? Approximately 80 grams – that is the equivalent of a bowl of mixed salad or three tablespoons of peas or carrots, half a fresh pepper, one medium tomato, seven cherry tomatoes, a medium-sized apple or orange.

2 Cut down on junk food and snacks as they are often high in sugar and fat and may be full of additives.

3 Cut back on processed food such as cakes and biscuits – again, they are likely to be high in sugar and fat.

4 Cut back on ready meals, take-aways, etc., which are often high in saturated fat.

5 Aim for more wholefoods – wholemeal bread, wholewheat pasta, wholegrain rice. These contain many important vitamins and minerals. They have a low glycaemic index (sometimes called the GI factor), which means a smaller rise in blood sugar – helping to avoid the see-sawing highs and lows that can adversely affect mood.

6 Eat two portions of fish a week, one of which should be oily like salmon or mackerel. Oily fish contains omega 3 fatty acids, which not only may help to reduce the risk of a fatal heart attack, but also improve the mood.

7 Eat more nuts and seeds. Brazil nuts, for example, are a good source of selenium – an antioxidant mineral that can help to improve the mood. Many people avoid nuts because they are high in fat and therefore high in calories, but most are high in healthier monounsaturated fats (associated with the heart-healthy Mediterranean diet) rather than the unhealthy saturated fats that raises cholesterol levels. Pumpkin seeds contain L-tryptophan, which may help improve the mood, while sesame seeds contain inositol, which may also be mood-enhancing.

8 Drink plenty of water – around eight glasses a day is ideal – as this will help to give more energy and flush out toxins. Tea and coffee does count towards your liquid intake, but they can be dehydrating – plus they contain caffeine, which can exacerbate irritability and anxiety. Plain water is better.

9 If low blood sugar is a problem, eat little and often. This is a good strategy for women who suffer from pre-menstrual syndrome.

10 Avoid alcohol. You should in any case drink no more than 2 to 3 units a day if you are a woman, and not more than 3 to 4 units

a day if you are a man. One problem is that while 1 unit is the equivalent of a 'pub measure', or small 1.24 ml glass of wine, many pubs serve wine in a bigger glass. In addition, in the case of wine, one unit is the equivalent of a 125 ml glass – but only if the wine is 9 per cent alcohol by volume (abv). Most wines are much stronger than this, so a large glass of 14 per cent wine could equal a massive 3.5 units, which is more than a woman's entire daily allowance is meant to be. Therefore it is easy to drink far more than the units recommended without even noticing. In addition, a woman's body is comprised of 10 per cent more fat and contains less fluid than a man's, so the concentration of alcohol in a woman's body is higher. Plus, the alcohol stays longer in the system before being metabolized. In other words, a woman may get drunk more quickly and alcohol will stay in her system longer than in a man's. Also, bear in mind that although alcohol is often regarded as a way of relaxing, in fact it is a depressant. Someone who has depression will feel better if they avoid alcohol.

More tips

If you suspect that food may be triggering your symptoms, one way to find out is to keep a 'Food Diary'. This means each day writing down exactly what you eat, and the time you eat it. You should also note how you feel, perhaps on a scale of 1–10, with regard to each symptom, e.g. feeling irritable, feeling sad, feeling angry and so on, again noting down the time. If you can see a particular pattern emerge it may highlight an intolerance to a certain food.

Changing one's diet is not easy – as anyone who has ever tried to lose weight will know! The key is to make small, achievable changes that can be sustained. That probably means making one change at a time – which will also make it easier to see if the change (e.g. cutting out chocolate) has had a positive effect.

Bear in mind that some changes – cutting out caffeine-containing foods such as chocolate, fizzy drinks and coffee – may produce withdrawal symptoms such as headaches or irritability, as well as cravings for the food concerned. This can tempt you to give in and go back to them, but if you persevere you may start to feel much better. It is hard to say how long it will take to wean oneself off a particular food – between one and two weeks is average.

Withdrawal symptoms are likely to be worse if you cut out a food overnight, so if this is a worry it could be done gradually instead. It is possible to have a food allergy or intolerance, but it is not nearly as common as people think. According to the Food Standards Agency, up to 40 per cent of people in the UK *think* they have a food allergy or intolerance, but the real figure is closer to 1 or 2 per cent. What is the difference between a food allergy and food intolerance? An allergy is when the body reacts to a harmless food and sees it as a threat. In response it activates the immune (defence) system. The body produces special antibodies in the blood to attack the 'invading' food and in turn this causes other blood cells to release chemicals such as histamine, which can cause a range of symptoms from rashes to wheeziness.

A food intolerance may cause the same symptoms as a food allergy, but occurs when the body cannot digest a food (e.g. as in lactose intolerance in dairy products) because it does not produce sufficient quantities of a vital enzyme or chemical. (Some allergies, especially allergies to nuts, can be life-threatening – if not treated immediately, anaphylactic shock can be fatal.)

In general, wheat, cows' milk, other dairy products, nuts, eggs, fish and shellfish, citrus and berry fruits and chocolate are some of the most common triggers – which are many of the foods that seem to trigger mood changes in some people.

It is possible to test for food allergies via a skin prick, blood test, or a carefully controlled, medically supervised elimination diet. But despite glossy advertisements to the contrary, food *intolerance* cannot be reliably diagnosed via skin, hair analysis, or other tests, though blood tests may offer some clues.

Exercise

There is a great deal of evidence that exercise is an incredibly useful treatment for depression. If someone you love has depression, this can seem an almost useless piece of information. After all, someone who is depressed may be lethargic, uncommunicative, with very poor motivation and so on. You might well wonder how you could ever encourage them to exercise when they do not seem able to get up out of a chair, or won't even go to the shops with you. So you are right to be sceptical.

On the other hand, there is so much evidence now that taking exercise really can alleviate anxiety and depression that it's worth looking at this. It is also an invaluable strategy for someone who is recovering from depression or someone vulnerable to depression. For example, studies have shown that exercise compares favourably to psychotherapy and cognitive therapy, and that significant improvements can be achieved within five weeks (with sessions of aerobic exercise such as brisk walking, three times a week for 20–30 minutes or more). Interestingly, it is thought that non-aerobic exercise (such as working with weights or yoga) is just as effective.

There are several possible reasons why exercise is useful. One theory is that it raises the levels of chemicals in our bodies called endorphins – which are known to be mood enhancers. But it also helps to make someone feel they are 'doing' something positive for themselves, and provides a period of time where all that person's concentration and thought goes into the exercise rather than worrying about something else. Exercising rhythmically can also be a kind of meditation, enabling you to 'switch off' from worries.

Researchers from Nottingham Trent University found that, after exercise, levels of a chemical known as phenylacetic acid are increased in the body by up to 77 per cent. There is evidence that levels of phenylacetic acid (and phenylethylamine, which converts to phenylacetic acid in the body and is known to be connected to mood) are low in people who are depressed.

Exercise also helps to 'use up' the adrenaline produced when we are stressed, which would otherwise circulate in the body and produce stress symptoms. Exercise also helps to relax the muscles; it promotes sounder sleep too, and really does seem to help to improve self-esteem. Aerobic exercise such as brisk walking is ideal, but any form of exercise is likely to be of benefit in improving mood – including gentler forms of exercise such as t'ai chi and yoga. So it looks likely that exercise helps to improve mood, and alleviate the symptoms of depression, for a wide variety of reasons.

The obvious difficulty here is that if the person you love who is depressed seems a million miles away from being able to attend an aerobics class, it seems pointless to recommend exercise. It may be beneficial, but if someone is totally lacking in motivation and enthusiasm it can seem a hopeless suggestion. There is no easy answer to this, and it would be silly to pretend there was. The best advice is to 'start small' and work on the assumption that every little helps. Anything is better than nothing, and even standing up and doing arm circles or dancing around the room to a record will help; a minor change may 'feed upon itself', and make moving up a notch to the next level a little easier next time (Tkachuk and Martin, 1999).

12

Could counselling help?

There has been a huge interest in counselling and psychotherapy in the past 20 years, and many people who have depression have found it enormously useful. There are many different types of counselling, and what suits one person will not suit another; but if someone feels they might benefit from counselling and can find the right counsellor for them, it could be a tremendous help.

Many doctors are now providing counselling services at the surgery free of charge, though there may be a waiting list. But this option would be well worth exploring as counselling can be expensive. Most counsellors operate a sliding scale of fees, so that the unwaged, students and those on a low income may be charged a little less.

What is the difference between counselling and psychotherapy? For many people, the terms are interchangeable. Both are 'talking treatments' based on the interaction that takes place between the client and the counsellor/psychotherapist. Strictly speaking, the term 'psychotherapy' is specifically associated with Freudian psychoanalysis, but although some practitioners call themselves psychotherapists they are not necessarily Freudian-trained. In general, psychotherapy tends to be a longer-term treatment than counselling, and is very much rooted in trying to understand the client's past and, particularly, how what is said in the therapy session itself reflects the client's unconscious motives. Some practitioners now offer 'brief psychotherapy', and this tends to be, as the name implies, a shorter, more focused type of psychotherapy.

Whichever type of therapy is chosen, sessions are set up in a disciplined way, with 'boundaries' to protect both client and therapist. From the outset, the therapist should discuss what is expected of the client and what they can expect in return. For example, the client is expected to turn up at a set time for a set period (usually 50 minutes or one hour) and to give notice if they can't attend. The essence of counselling is that clients are not given 'advice', but helped to understand themselves better and find their own solutions. Counsellors do, however, offer insights and aim to empower and enable clients by carefully listening to what is said – and often offering clients the opportunity to look in detail at patterns of thinking that may in some way be holding them back. The counselling session is often a really good opportunity for a client to explore how they might think or act differently in a variety of situations, look at past situations in a different way, or cope with difficult emotions like anger. But counsellors generally aim to give their clients what they call 'unconditional positive regard' – a kind of unconditional, non-judgemental acceptance and empathy – so that the counsellor aims to understand the client's point of view, no matter what. The counselling session is meant to be a 100 per cent safe place where a client can say anything they want (excluding the confession of a major crime such as murder), knowing that the counsellor will not judge them, will not reject them but will understand them, accept them, and try to help them. Confidentiality is guaranteed, although a counsellor may discuss aspects with their own 'supervisor'.

There are many different types of counselling, such as person-centred, psychodynamic and cognitive therapy; you can read more about these on page 123.

How to find a counsellor

A good start is to contact the British Association for Counselling and Psychotherapy (BACP), the British Association of Behavioural and Cognitive Psychotherapies (BABCP) or the UK Council for Psychotherapy (UKCP) (in the UK) as these organizations will be able to provide you with a list of counsellors and psychotherapists in your own area (see Useful Addresses). You would then receive a list with contact details, and some clues as to how the therapist works and any particular specialties they have. Some specialize in dealing with people who have work problems, some specialize in dealing with people who have been abused as a child, some work mainly with couples, others with children or adolescents, and so on.

As noted at the beginning of this chapter, there may be long waiting lists for NHS-funded counselling and psychotherapy. Students often have good access to counselling services at colleges and universities, and some large employers now offer workplace counselling.

Many voluntary organizations such as Cruse Bereavement Care (for those who have suffered a bereavement), Victim Support (for those who have been the victim of a crime) and Relate (for individuals or couples with relationship difficulties) also offer counselling. Contact these organizations direct (see Useful Addresses) to see what is available. Also, there are many other voluntary groups and charities who specialize in specific issues or problems and offer counselling, or who can put you in touch with counsellors with specialist knowledge on areas such as abortion, HIV, adoption, sexual abuse, lesbian and gay problems, and so on.

If you are paying for counselling or psychotherapy, you may be offered a reduced rate, or even a free first session, so that you and the therapist can decide if you can 'work together'. This gives both sides the chance to size each other up. The counselling sessions may take place in a room that the therapist rents in a natural healing centre, or in the therapist's own home; generally, counselling rooms are functional without too many of the therapist's belongings around to distract the client.

At the moment, anyone can call himself or herself a counsellor, yet have very little training – some may have only been on a couple of weekend courses or may even have taken a simple correspondence course! So it is important to find someone who is properly trained – ask about their qualifications, how long their training was, and with whom. A good counsellor or psychotherapist will not be afraid to answer these questions – indeed, they will be pleased they were asked. Obviously it is important for any client willing to part with his or her money for counselling to ensure that the counsellor is properly trained. The counsellor should tell you if he or she is a member of a professional body, such as the BACP. All members of the BACP are bound by what's called the 'Ethical Framework for Good Practice in Counselling and Psychotherapy'. This Code is wide ranging, and primarily designed to safeguard clients' interests – the BACP has a Complaints Procedure which can lead to the expulsion of members for breaches of the Code.

This means the therapist will have signed up to specific rules and regulations and ways of working that are designed to protect the client. The counsellor should also be having 'supervision' – that is, regular sessions with a counsellor of their own. Many people wrongly assume that 'being in supervision' means that the counsellor is somehow not qualified enough to be a proper counsellor in their own right, but this is not the case – being in supervision shows that the counsellor is a professional and is taking their job very seriously indeed.

Typically, a client would attend a counselling session once a week for a set number of weeks to be discussed with the counsellor. It is not considered to be the 'done thing' to just not turn up for a counselling session without warning, to try to chop and change counselling times without a very good reason, or to stop going for counselling without talking it through with the counsellor first. Counsellors also like to 'make a good ending' rather than stop abruptly. The professional contract between client and therapist often means that the client is expected to pay for missed sessions unless adequate notice has been given, or agreed at the outset. Some people find a short number of sessions – say five or six – is sufficient to get them through a particular crisis; others find a longer stint of a year or more most beneficial. Psychotherapy may involve one or more sessions a week and is usually for at least a year or more.

Can counselling help someone who is depressed?

Counselling can help most people – though it may not be appropriate where a person is severely depressed or suffering from a mental health disorder such as schizophrenia. A study by BACP published in December 2002 in the *British Medical Journal* showed that the most effective help for the treatment of depression lasting less than a year is counselling, either person-centred or cognitive therapy.

If the cause of depression is related to a specific event such as bereavement, or a specific problem such as difficulties with a particular relationship, then it can be particularly useful – research shows that where depression is of less than six months' duration, counselling can be more effective, and work more quickly, than antidepressants.

What happens in a counselling session?

This very much depends on how the therapist works and the particular discipline they have trained under (see below). Initially it is often a huge relief to be able to talk to someone in confidence and tell them how you feel. Sometimes, though, the partners of those having counselling can feel left out or worry the counselling is doing more harm than good. If you find yourself in this situation it is undeniably hard as obviously you cannot find out what is going on! To a certain extent, you have to trust that what goes on in the counselling sessions is for the benefit of the person you love. You might want to let them know that they can talk to you about their therapy – but on the other hand it's pointless feeling upset if they don't want to tell you anything. Counselling is meant to be completely confidential, and no one should feel obliged to disclose anything about what goes on in a session, even to their partner or parent.

Questions that could be asked at an initial counselling session

- What type of counselling do you offer?
- Are you a member of any professional body?
- Does it have a Code of Ethics and Practice you abide by?
- How long have you been a counsellor?
- What are your qualifications?
- Have you counselled other people who are experiencing depression?
- How much do you charge per session?
- How do you prefer to be paid?
- How long is each session?
- What happens if I can't make a session, or have to cancel at short notice?
- Can I telephone you between sessions?
- Will our sessions be 100 per cent confidential?
- Will sessions be tape-recorded and, if so, who would listen to the tapes and what would happen to them?
- What should I do if I am worried that the sessions aren't going very well?

Types of therapy

Person-centred counselling

Sometimes called the 'humanistic' approach, this branch of therapy was originally developed by Carl Rogers. The therapy starts from the premise that the client has vast potential for change, growth, development and fulfilment. The counsellor helps the client to reach their potential by offering genuineness, total acceptance, or what counsellors call 'unconditional positive regard' and empathy. But what does such jargon mean in practice?

The idea is for a client to feel comfortable enough to say anything they want – and feel confident that the therapist will understand, accept what they say, explore their feelings further, and so on. The great thing about person-centred counselling is that clients often feel really listened to and heard, and may feel for the first time that they are being taken seriously – so it can be an enormous relief. The counsellor won't try to censor what the client wants to say, so it can be a wonderful release to feel you can open up and say every little thing you want to say. The counsellor won't be afraid to offer interpretations, insights, hunches, and even guide a client as to different ways they might approach a certain situation or relationship, but they won't offer specific advice. The emphasis tends to be on what's happening in the client's life at the moment rather than an over-reliance on talking about their childhood and past, although in practice this is often relevant and may well be addressed at length.

Many different types of therapy are rooted in the person-centred approach, including transactional analysis (TA), Gestalt therapy, psychodrama, existential therapy, feminist therapy, psychosynthesis and transpersonal therapy.

Case history: George

I had suffered from mild depression for about three months before I went to see a transpersonal counsellor. I wasn't sure what to expect, and thought it might be some kind of mystical thing – especially as there were a few mystical-type posters in the therapist's room and she always had a candle burning. But it was fantastic. She was so good at understanding what I said, and I never felt judged – even on the things I felt most guilty about.

Although the boundaries of the session were always just so – finishing on the dot of time and having to pay for any session I missed and so on – I felt she really wanted the best for me. I trusted her absolutely. It's hard to be specific about what changed inside me. I think she helped me just get everything I wanted to say out, and that in itself was brilliant. I said things to her I could never say to my mother or my wife. I just reached a point where I felt ready to move on. I don't know how it helped, but I am sure it did.

Psychodynamic counselling or psychotherapy

Although the term is used differently by different people, psychodynamic counsellors tend to belong more to the Freudian school, working from the premise that our unconscious reveals itself in dreams, slips of the tongue, remarks we may say but then claim we didn't mean, physical symptoms, and so on. The client is encouraged to express everything they are feeling and thinking in order to uncover unconscious thoughts and have insights into how the past impinges on present behaviour – the idea is that gradually as you become more aware, you can shake off the past and outdated ways of thinking, and free yourself up to be happier in the present. This type of therapy tends to be long term – some people find it very helpful, others find it less useful.

Cognitive behaviour therapy (CBT)

Cognitive behaviour therapy was developed as a treatment for depression in the mid 1950s and early 1960s. It works on the principle that our feelings stem from the thoughts we choose to have and the messages we give to ourselves. At its simplest level, cognitive therapy suggests that by *changing* our thoughts, the way we think about things, and the messages we give to ourselves, we can literally change our feelings, and transform our mood. It sounds ridiculously simplistic, but research shows it can be effective. Cognitive behaviour therapists are less interested in delving in detail into a person's past, and more concerned with what a person's problems are today and helping them to overcome them. A cognitive behaviour therapist is more interested in what the present problem is, not what might have caused it. It tends to be

124

very effective with problems such as anxiety, obsessive-compul-
sive disorders, and phobias too.

Cognitive behaviour therapy starts from the premise that we tend
to confuse feelings with facts and are prone to distorted kinds of
thinking. Someone who has had a series of unsuccessful relationships, for example, may wrongly start to believe they are
unlovable.

So what does cognitive therapy involve? The therapist aims to
help a client to overcome faulty thinking, such as over-generaliza-
tion about people or situations, all-or-nothing thinking, or blink-
ered thinking that homes in on the negative and always ignores
the positive aspect of any given situation. The therapist will
challenge any examples of 'faulty thinking' that might be holding
the person back. For example, if the client says 'I'm no good at
anything' or 'everything is hopeless', the therapist will unpick the
reality behind such statements and help the client see that such
generalizations are simply not true. There are things the person is
good at and there are almost certainly some positive things in the
person's life. The therapist will help a client to understand how
such negative thoughts influence feelings and mood, and help them
to latch on to a more accurate and logical way of thinking. The
therapist will also help a client to devise more effective coping
strategies to make them feel better, set 'goals', and even
'homework'.

Case history: Rob

I suffered from mild depression for many years before I was
referred by a new doctor to a cognitive behaviour therapist. One
of the reasons I so often slipped into a depressive state was my
constant drive for perfectionism – not just in myself, but in
others too. When I fell short of my own expectations I would
mentally beat myself up over it, think about how I had failed,
and ultimately would be almost paralysed with guilt, self-
reproach and misery. It sounds so simple, but one of the
techniques I learnt in cognitive therapy was that instead of living
my life expecting 100 per cent of myself and others, I started
expecting only 70 per cent. That gave me a breathing space, a
margin of error in which to fail instead of be perfect all the time.
Quite often I found that I did better than the 70 per cent I started

125

to expect of myself. It meant on a daily basis that instead of worrying about failing I could relax just a bit, and as often or not pleasantly surprise myself.

It took away a lot of the tension and anxiety I had been feeling, it also gave me a more realistic goal to aim for, and a better chance of succeeding. Instead of feeling frozen with fear half the time, I began to enjoy life a bit more. And it had a knock-on effect on my relationships with family and friends too – instead of expecting everything to be 100 per cent perfect all the time, I built in a margin of error for others too, so when things weren't perfect it was easier to handle and not over-react. I'm not saying this happened overnight, but it was as though someone had clicked a switch in me. It was a completely new way of looking at things and improved so many aspects of my everyday life.

The client emerges from cognitive therapy with a series of problem-solving and coping techniques that they can apply to every kind of crisis and situation from minor irritations and vague worries, dilemmas, setbacks and feelings such as low self-esteem, to major emotional challenges and situations such as divorce and bereavement. One attraction of cognitive therapy to many people is that it tends to be contained – often lasting no longer than six months.

Many people are resistant to cognitive therapy because it's scary to let go of ideas and patterns of behaviour we already have. We all get locked into patterns of thinking and it is strangely uncomfortable to face the possibility that our thoughts may be irrational, even if the pay-off is that by changing our thoughts we could feel happier. If someone feels really down, then that feeling will seem 100 per cent realistic and appropriate. Learning to 'reframe' thoughts can help pull someone out of depression – what's more, someone who is depressed can be taught the techniques so that, much of the time, they can get into the habit of helping themselves. In terms of efficacy, studies show that cognitive therapy may be as effective as antidepressants, if not more so (Rush *et al.*, 1977).

Another type of cognitive therapy is known as rational emotive behaviour therapy (REBT). It is similar to cognitive therapy and focuses on how a person's thinking upsets them emotionally. The person is then taught to identify self-defeating thoughts and replace them with more realistic ones that are less likely to make them depressed or unhappy.

To find a qualified counsellor, ask your doctor or look at the Useful Addresses section on page 135.

13

The role of complementary therapies

There are hundreds of different complementary or alternative therapies, ranging from those now considered to be mainstream – such as homoeopathy and acupuncture – to more alternative therapies such as Reiki. Not all doctors are sympathetic to complementary therapies, and some are antagonistic towards even the most mainstream of them.

It is not difficult to see why the medical profession has been slow to accept complementary medicine. Most of what doctors are taught in medical schools is based on scientific research and clinical trials – evidence-based medicine. So we shouldn't be surprised if they are keen to question anecdotal evidence. Unfortunately, there are relatively few scientific studies looking at whether specific complementary therapies may be of value in treating depression or relieving some of its symptoms.

In the case of depression, medical help should always be sought; and if complementary therapies are to play a role, then it is likely to be in addition to conventional medicine.

One attraction of many complementary therapies is that they offer a holistic approach – treating the whole person. Many of the therapies focus on the idea of 'balance' and 'energy'. The idea is that there is a state of natural balance within the body, and that when this balance is disturbed, illness can result. When balance is achieved, then the body has a better chance of healing itself.

There are no guarantees or clear-cut answers with complementary therapies. What seems to be of benefit to one person may not be to another. It is a question of seeing if it works for you.

Different types of complementary therapies

Complementary therapies that may be useful in alleviating anxiety or stress include:

Acupuncture

Acupuncture is an ancient Chinese therapy widely used in mainstream Chinese medicine, and it has become increasingly popular in the Western world.

An acupuncturist uses needles to stimulate particular points on the 'meridians' (invisible channels) in the body. The procedure doesn't hurt, but you may feel a tingling or numbness.

According to the principles behind acupuncture, energy or 'chi' is thought to flow along these channels to and from our various organs, maintaining physical, emotional and mental well-being. If the flow of chi is disrupted, or perhaps blocked because of an emotional upset, illness can result. The aim of acupuncture is to stimulate the flow of chi again to create greater harmony and balance within the body, and kick-start the body's own healing abilities.

While the concept of 'chi' may be dismissed in conventional Western medicine, it does appear to be effective for some people – in the treatment of stress, for example.

Aromatherapy

Aromatherapy is the use of aromatic essential oils extracted from different plants. Each oil is said to have unique properties, which can be used to relax, soothe, energize or rebalance the body, while other oils are noted for their healing ability – for example, as anti-inflammatory agents. The oils are very concentrated – it takes several kilos of lavender to produce a very small bottle of essential oil. The oils can be used in different ways – for example in the bath, as a massage oil, or as an inhalation. When used for massage, oils must be mixed with a 'base' or carrier oil such as sweet almond oil. You must consult a qualified aromatherapist before using oils on children, or if you think you might be pregnant. Some oils should be avoided if you have certain medical complaints such as epilepsy.

Homoeopathy

The basic idea of homoeopathy is to try to stimulate the body's own healing potential by trying to cure like with like – administering a minute, diluted dose of a substance that in a large dose in a well person would mimic the symptoms of the disease the practitioner is aiming to relieve.

Massage

This forms the basis of many therapies, such as aromatherapy, but is of great value in its own right. A relaxing massage can help float away minor tensions. It is particularly useful if you are not in a relationship (and even if you are!) as the power of touch can be very therapeutic.

Meditation

Many people believe regular meditation is a good de-stressor. You can pay to learn specific techniques such as Transcendental Meditation (TM), or just have a go at home using simple techniques that anyone can try. It is a shame that meditation is sometimes portrayed as being shrouded in mystique – it really is something anyone can do. Set aside about 20 minutes, sit quietly, notice your breathing, and the rise and fall of your stomach as you breathe. If it helps, focus on a candle flame or repeat a made-up word or 'mantra'. At first your mind will wander, but that's OK – just gently refocus each time. Notice your breathing becoming gradually more relaxed and deeper – if you find yourself sighing it's a good sign as it shows you are relaxing properly. Don't allow outside noises to worry you; just notice them, accept them, and carry on.

Visualization

Combined with meditation, this can be a powerful tool. You can either try on your own, visualizing a relaxing scene such as walking by a stream or lying in a meadow for example, or attend a guided meditation/visualization where a leader takes you on a 'journey' as you listen to their words and imagine what they describe.

How to find a therapist

If you are interested in trying a complementary therapy, discuss it with your doctor first to be on the safe side. There are around 45,000 complementary practitioners in the UK, but no one single register or Code of Practice. Some therapies have more than one governing body, which can make choosing a therapist quite tricky. It's a good idea to keep your ears open – going on personal recommendation is always a good idea. The best approach is to find out as much as you can about the training the therapist has undergone, how much experience they have, and what Code of Practice they abide by. If the therapist is unwilling to answer questions about their training, then go to someone else. Be wary of those who say they trained for 'five years' – this may simply mean they attended one weekend course every year! *So beware.* It's also sensible to choose a practitioner you feel comfortable with.

Avoid any therapist who tries to make a diagnosis or who guarantees their treatment will cure you. Do not, under any circumstances, give up taking prescribed medication or abandon conventional treatment without fully discussing it with your doctor and/or specialist.

You can get further advice from the Foundation for Integrated Medicine, the Institute for Complementary Medicine or the British Complementary Medicine Association (see Useful Addresses).

St John's Wort

This herbal remedy has attracted as much interest as Prozac and is said to be used extensively in Europe, especially Germany, as a firstline treatment for mild to moderate depression. St John's Wort (the Latin botanical name is *Hypericum perforatum*) is a common perennial flowering plant native to Europe, Asia and North Africa, but is now grown extensively in North America.

This particular herbal remedy for depression, which is derived from the plant's flowering buds, has now been evaluated by over 30 scientific studies and the results are very promising. The results of one meta-analysis (an analysis of 23 clinical studies involving a total of over 1,700 patients) suggest that standardized St John's Wort extract is more effective than a placebo, but also just as effective as the antidepressant drugs to which it was compared – and with fewer side-effects. It is not yet known exactly how it works. One theory is that it may inhibit the breakdown of serotonin, one of the neurotransmitters responsible for controlling mood, or increase the effect of serotonin in the brain. Other research suggests that it contains the hormone melatonin, which is also known to promote a good mood. St John's Wort has also been found to be of use in treating Seasonal Affective Disorder (SAD).

You should check with a qualified medical herbalist and/or a doctor before taking St John's Wort. Although the remedy is tolerated well by most people, there are some contraindications – and someone who is already taking prescription antidepressants or other medications should seek advice first. There is evidence of an adverse reaction when taken at the same time as SSRI antidepressants (research from MIND).

In the USA, a four-year study by the US National Institutes of Health (NIH) is underway to compare St John's Wort both with a placebo, and with the SSRI antidepressant citalopram (US National Institutes of Health, 2002).

Bear in mind that new studies are being conducted all the time, so seeking advice is essential to get the most up-to-date information. The use of a herbal remedy like St John's Wort is not a substitute for other medical treatment, and it is not advised that you self-diagnose depression or use this (or any other herbal remedy) to self-treat.

Further Reading

MIND produce a superb range of factsheets, booklets and other publications at very reasonable prices. For a catalogue of publications from MIND, send an A4 SAE to:

MIND Mail Order, 15–19 Broadway, London E15 4BQ
Tel: 020 8221 9666, or see *www.mind.org.uk*

The Royal College of Psychiatrists also offer an excellent range of factsheets, leaflets and other publications. For information, contact the Royal College of Psychiatrists, 17 Belgrave Square, London SW1X 8PG.
Tel: 020 7235 2351, or see *www.rcpsych.ac.uk*

Useful books

Carlson, Richard, *Stop Thinking and Start Living*, Thorsons, 1997.
Dryden, Dr Windy, and Feltham, Colin, *Counselling and Psychotherapy*, Sheldon Press, 1995.
Freeman, Chris (ed.), *The ECT Handbook*, the Royal College of Psychiatrists, 1995.
Gilbert, Paul, *Counselling for Depression*, Sage, 2000.
Gilbert, Paul, *Overcoming Depression. A Self-help Guide Using Cognitive Behavioural Techniques*, Robinson, 1997.
Goodyer, Ian M., *Unipolar Depression. A Lifespan Perspective*, Oxford University Press, 2003.
Kabat-Zinn, Jon, *Full Catastrophe Living*, Piatkus, 1990.
McDermott, Ian, and Shircore, Ian, *Manage Yourself, Manage Your Life*, Piatkus, 1999.
Milligan, Spike, and Clare, Anthony, *Depression and How to Survive It*, Arrow, 1994.
Murray Parkes, Colin, *Bereavement Studies of Grief in Adult Life*, Pelican, 1972.

Rowe, Dorothy, *Depression: The Way out of Your Prison*, Routledge & Kegan Paul, 1983.

Sapolsky, Robert M., *Why Zebras Don't Get Ulcers*, W. H. Freeman & Co., 1998.

Wolpert, Lewis, *Malignant Sadness*, Faber & Faber, 1999.

Useful Addresses

Age Concern
Astral House, 1268 London Road, London SW16 4ER
Tel: 020 8765 7200
Helpline 0800 009 966
www.ace.org.uk

Association for Postnatal Illness
145 Dawes Road, London SW6 7EB
Tel: 020 7386 0868
www.apni.org

British Association for Behavioural and Cognitive Psychotherapies
PO Box 9, Accrington BB5 2GD
Tel: 01254 875277
www.babcp.com

British Association for Counselling and Psychotherapy
1 Regent Place, Rugby, Warwickshire CV21 2PJ
Tel: 0870 443 5252
www.counselling.co.uk

British Complementary Medicine Association
Kensington House, 33 Imperial Square, Cheltenham GL50 1QZ
Tel: 01242 519911
www.bcma.co.uk

British Holistic Medical Association
59 Lansdowne Place, Hove, East Sussex BN3 1FL
Tel: 01273 725951
www.bhma.org
(Can supply a list of practitioners.)

Carers UK
20–25 Glasshouse Yard, London EC1A 4JT
Tel: 020 7490 8818
Carers line: 0808 808 7777
www.carersonline.org.uk

Crossroads – Caring for Carers
10 Regent Place, Rugby, Warwickshire CV21 2PN
Tel: 01788 573653
www.carers.org.uk
(Provides respite help for carers.)

Cruse Bereavement Care
126 Sheen Road, Richmond, Surrey TW9 1UR
Tel: 020 8939 9530
Helpline: 0870 167 1677
www.crusebereavementcare.org.uk

Depression Alliance
35 Westminster Bridge Road, London SE1 7JB
Tel: 020 7633 0557
Helpline: 020 8768 0123
www.depressionalliance.org

Fellowship of Depressives Anonymous
Box FDA Self-help, Nottingham, Ormiston House, 32–36 Pelham
Street, Nottingham NG1 2EG
Info line: 01702 433838
www.depressionanon.co.uk

Foundation for Integrated Medicine
International House, 59 Compton Road, London N1 2YT
Tel: 020 7688 1881
www.fimed.org
(Provides details about governing bodies for individual therapies,
but cannot supply names of individual practitioners.)

Institute for Complementary Medicine
PO Box 194, London SE16 7QZ
Tel: 020 7237 5165
www.icmedicine.co.uk
(For information on complementary medicine and practitioners.)

Manic Depression Fellowship (MDF)
Castle Works, 21 St Georges Road, London SE1 6ES
Tel: 020 7793 2600
www.mdf.org.uk

Meet-a-Mum Association (MAMA)
See *www.mama.org.uk*
(Phone numbers may change, so website is the best point of contact.)

MIND (National Association for Mental Health)
15–19 Broadway, London E15 3BQ
Tel: 020 8519 2122
www.mind.org.uk

National Association for Premenstrual Syndrome (NAPS)
41 Old Road, East Peckham, Kent TN13 5AP
Tel: 0870 777 2178
www.pms.org.uk

National Debtline
318 Summer Lane, Birmingham B19 3RL
Freephone: 0808 808 4000
www.nationaldebtline.co.uk

NHS Direct
Tel: 0845 46 47

Pain Society
9 Bedford Square, London WC1B 3RA
Tel: 020 7636 2750
(Please write for information about pain clinics or treatments.)

Patients Association
PO Box 935, Harrow, Middlesex HA1 3YJ
Tel: 020 8423 9111
Helpline: 08456 084455
(Can help in a variety of ways, including information on how to make a complaint and how to gain access to your medical records.)

Relate
Herbert Gray College, Little Church Street, Rugby, Warwickshire CV21 3AP
Tel: 01788 573 241
www.relate.org.uk

Rethink Severe Mental Illness (formerly the National Schizophrenia Fellowship)
28 Castle Street, Kingston-upon-Thames, Surrey KT1 1SS
Advice line: 020 8974 6814
www.rethink.org
(Aims to improve the lives of everyone affected by severe mental illness.)

SAD Association
PO Box 989, Steyning BN44 3HG
www.sada.org.uk

Samaritans
Helpline: 08457 909090
www.samaritans.org.uk

Stroke Association, Stroke House
240 City Road, London EC1V 2PR
Tel: 020 7566 0300
Helpline: 0845 30 33 100
www.stroke.org.uk

Survivors' Poetry
Diorama Arts Centre, 34 Osnaburgh Street, London NW1 3ND
Tel: 020 7916 5317
www.groups.msn.com/survivorspoetry.org.uk

United Kingdom Council for Psychotherapy
167–169 Great Portland Street, London W1W 5PF
Tel: 020 7436 3002
www.psychotherapy.org.uk

Victim Support
Cranmer House, 39 Brixton Road, London SW9 6DZ
Tel: 020 7735 9166
Helpline: 0845 3030 900
www.victimsupport.com

Young Minds
102–108 Clerkenwell Road, London EC1M 5SA
Helpline: 0800 018 2138
www.youngminds.org.uk
(For parents or those concerned with the mental health of children
and younger people.)

References

Asarnow, J. R., and Bates, S. (1988) 'Depression in child psychiatric inpatients: cognitive and attributional patterns', *Journal of Abnormal Child Psychology*, 16, 601–15, in Goodyer (2003), chapter 3.

BBC (2003) News, 9 April.

Benbow, S. (2001) 'ECT in the treatment of depression in older patients', in Curran *et al.* (eds) (2001), chapter 5.

Birmaher, B., *et al.* (1996) 'Childhood and adolescent depression: a review of the past 10 years – part 1', *Journal of the American Academy of Child and Adolescent Psychiatry*, 35, 1427–39, in Goodyer (2003), chapter 3.

Birmaher, B., and Rozel, J. S. (2003) 'Unipolar depression – a lifespan perspective: "The school age child"', in Goodyer (2003), chapter 3.

Bjelland, I., *et al.* (2003) 'Folate and depression', *Psychotherapy and Psychosomatics*, 72, 59–60.

BNF (*British National Formulary*) (2002) 'The drug treatment of depression in primary care', 44, September.

Brown, G. W., and Harris, T. (1978) *The Social Origins of Depression: A Study of Psychiatric Disorder in Women*, London, Tavistock Publications.

Curran, S., *et al.* (eds) (2001) *Practical Management of Depression in Older People*, London, Arnold.

Davison, G. C., and Neale, John M. (1998) *Abnormal Psychology*, 7th edn, John Wiley & Sons.

Emslie, G. J., *et al.* (1998) 'Fluoxetine in child and adolescent depression: acute and maintenance treatment', *Depress. Anxiety*, 7, 32–9, in Goodyer (2003), chapter 3.

Flint, A. J. (1992) 'The optimum duration of antidepressant treatment in the elderly', *International Journal of Geriatric Psychiatry*, 7, 617–19.

Geddes, J., *et al.* (2000) 'Depressive disorders in clinical evidence', Issue 4, BMJ Publishing Group, London, as cited in *BNF* (2002).

Geddes, J. (2003) in *The Lancet*, 361, 799–808.
Gershon, E. S. (1990) 'Genetics', in Goodwin, F. K., and Jamison, K. R. (eds) *Manic Depressive Illness*, New York, Oxford University Press, as cited in Davison and Neale (1998).
Gilbert, P. (2000) *Counselling for Depression*, Sage.
Gill, D., and Hatcher, S. (1999) 'Antidepressant drugs in depressed patients who also have a physical illness', as cited in Curran *et al.* (eds) (2001).
Goodyer, I. M., *et al.* (1997) 'Short-term outcome of major depression: 1. Comorbidity and severity at presentation as predictors of persistent disorder', *Journal of the American Academy of Child and Adolescent Psychiatry*, 36, 179–87, in Goodyer (2003), chapter 3.
Goodyer, I. M. (2003) *Unipolar Depression. A Lifespan Perspective*, Oxford University Press.
Goodyer, I. M. (2003) 'Characteristics of unipolar depressions', in Goodyer (2003), chapter 1.
Holmes, T. H., and Rahe, R. H. (1967) 'The Social Readjustment Rating Scale', *Journal of Psychosomatic Research*, 11, 213–18.
Kovacs, M., *et al.* (1984) 'Depressive disorders in childhood: I. a longitudinal perspective study of characteristics and recovery', *Archives of General Psychiatry*, 41, 229–37, in Goodyer (2003), chapter 3.
Kovacs, M., *et al.* (1984) 'Depressive disorders in childhood: II. a longitudinal study of the risk for a subsequent major depression', *Archives of General Psychiatry*, 41, 643–9, in Goodyer (2003), chapter 3.
Kovacs, M., *et al.* (1989) 'Depressive disorders in childhood: IV. a longitudinal study of comorbidity with and risk for anxiety disorders', *Archives of General Psychiatry*, 46, 776–82, in Goodyer (2003), chapter 8.
Lipowski, Z. J., *et al.* (1994) 'The 24 hour profiles of cortisol, prolactin and growth hormone secretion in mania', *Archives of General Psychiatry*, 51, 616–24, as cited in Davison and Neale (1998).
Martin, P. (1997) *The Sickening Mind*, Flamingo.
McCauley, E., *et al.* (1993) 'Depression in young people: initial presentation and clinical course', *Journal of the American*

REFERENCES

Academy of Child and Adolescent Psychiatry, 32, 714–22, in Goodyer (2003), chapter 3.

McGee, R., and Williams, S. (1988) 'A longitudinal study of depression in nine year old children', *Journal of the American Academy of Child and Adolescent Psychiatry*, 27, 342–8, in Goodyer (2003), chapter 3.

McGuffin, P., and Katz, R. (1989) 'The genetics of depression and manic-depressive illness', *British Journal of Psychiatry*, 155, 294–304, as cited in Milligan and Clare (1994).

Milligan, Spike, and Clare, Anthony (1994) *Depression and How to Survive It*, Arrow.

Mulley, G. (2001) 'Depression in physically ill older patients', in Curran *et al.* (eds) (2001), chapter 7.

National Institute of Mental Health (see *www.nimh.nih.gov*).

O'Brien, J., and Thomas, A. (2003) 'Later life', in Goodyer (2003), chapter 7.

Observer (2003), 13 April, p. 715: 'Postnatal depression is a form of mourning, say experts', by Jo Revill.

Paykel, E. S., and Kennedy, N. (2003) 'Depression in mid life', in Goodyer (2003), chapter 6.

Persaud, R. (1997) *Staying Sane*, Metro Books.

Poznanski, E. O., *et al.* (1976) 'Childhood depression: a longitudinal perspective', *Journal of the American Academy of Child Psychiatry*, 15, 491–501, in Goodyer (2003), chapter 3.

Rush, A. J., *et al.* (1977) 'Comparative efficacy of cognitive therapy and pharmacotherapy in the treatment of depressed outpatients', *Cognitive Therapy and Research*, vol. 1, no. 1, March, 17–38, as cited in Burns, D. D., *Feeling Good. The New Mood Therapy*, Avon Books /Whole Care Health.

Sarafino, Edward P. (1990) *Health Psychology*, John Wiley & Sons.

Seligman, M. E. P. (1975) *On Depression, Development and Death*, San Francisco, Freeman, as cited in Sarafino (1990), p. 117.

Tkachuk, Gregg A., and Martin, Garry L. (1999) 'Exercise therapy for patients with psychiatric disorders: research and clinical implications', *American Psychological Association Profession Psychology: Research and Practice Journal*, Department of Psychology, University of Manitoba, June, vol. 30, no. 3,

275–82. Also, see *www.50plushealth.co.uk*, 2001 research archive.

Wattis, J. P. (2001) 'Getting the measure of depression in old age', in Curran *et al.* (eds) (2001), chapter 1.

Williams, J. J., *et al.* (2002) 'Is this patient clinically depressed?' *JAMA*, 2002, 287, 1160–1170, and as cited in Bandolier, May 2002; see *www.jr2.ox.ac.uk/bandolier/band99/b99-6.html* *Bandolier* is a print and internet journal, produced via Oxford University, for healthcare professionals and consumers. It reviews evidence-based research to report on particular treatments or diseases.) Also, American Psychiatric Association (1994) *Diagnostic and Statistical Manual of Mental Disorders*, 4th edn, Washington, DC.

Wilson, S., and Curran, S. (2001), 'The pharmacological treatment of depression in older people', in Curran *et al.* (eds) (2001).

World Health Report (2001) *Mental Health: New Understanding, New Hope.*

Index